QUICK FIXES

303

Ways to Help Yourself BEFORE the Therapist Arrives

Marylou Hughes

Crossroad • New York

1993

The Crossroad Publishing Company
370 Lexington Avenue, New York, NY 10017

Printed in the United States of America

Library of Congress Cataloging-in-Publication Data

Hughes, Marylou.
    Quick fixes : 303 ways to help yourself before the therapist
arrives / Marylou Hughes.
        p.   cm.
    ISBN 0-8245-1273-1
    1. Stress (Psychology)   2. Adjustment (Psychology)   3. Stress
management.   I. Title.
BF575.S75H836   1993
158'.1—dc20   92-37822
                                                          CIP

Book design and illustrations by James E. Barry

To
Fran and Ike Stormer

Acknowledgments to
Fred Coonce

CONTENTS

INTRODUCTION

QUICK FIXES are often not permanent cures. The quick fix is the Band-Aid approach. Cures often take more work, more time, and on occasion, more pain to allow one to connect emotionally with past trauma and exit psychologically healthier. Nevertheless, until the commitment is made to strive for healing or to take the distressing steps that lead to change, comfort is possible. This book will provide you with many instant and easy activities and processes that will help you feel better, improve your circumstances, and bring relief. Some of these are deceptively simple, but nevertheless, they are effective. Many are quick, simple, and useful and they are part of the process that leads to feelings of well-being which will help you change your life for the better. Quick fixes can be part of permanent and beneficial habits.

• HOW TO USE THIS BOOK •

The contents list is the book's divisions by problem areas. Use this list as a reference to find the help you need. Try several of the suggestions, picking and choosing to find those that you feel able to do and that seem to assist you in getting better. Don't rule out an exercise because it sounds too easy or too hard. The easy ones are helpful. The one that seems alien to you may be just what you need. Give it a chance. Every proposal in this book has been designed to achieve positive results. None will do you any harm, and all have been used by others who want to feel and act better. If any procedure produces inexplicable anxiety or distress, it is a sign that you need more than a quick fix. You probably experience unexplainable pain in other situations in your life too. Make a note of this and get professional help from an accredited psychotherapist.

Although the procedures are listed by problem area, do not hesitate to look under related topics for ideas. Stress and anxiety are closely related, as are worry and shyness. Relaxation exercises are helpful for all problems. Most of them can be found in Chapter 1, the quick fixes for anxiety section.

This is a self-help book. So help yourself while improving yourself!

QUICK
FIXES

Chapter ONE

ANXIETY

• SYMPTOMS •

ANXIETY CAN RANGE from mild discomfort to a full-blown physical reaction that makes you think you are going to die.

Anxiety is a normal reaction to the unknown, to risk, and to various situations in which you put yourself on the line, such as when you perform publicly, meet bosses and dignitaries, and when you are being judged or scrutinized. You can get nervous about anything, even writing a check (particularly a large one) or eating with friends.

Normal tension can cause your hands to sweat, your body to feel hot or chilled, internal shaking, rapid heartbeat, and temporary amnesia. You may be unable to recall your name. You know what is making you nervous. When the situation is over your anxiety subsides, even though you can conjure up anxious feelings when you relive it in your mind.

Ann hated having to speak in a group. Whenever people introduced themselves in turn, she was barely able to vocalize by the time they got to her. Her heart beat loudly, her voice caught in her throat, she could not look at anyone. This was anxiety, but it was fleeting, and it was related to a specific incident.

Anxiety symptoms can be more severe. They can include stomach upset, and an inability to breathe, as well as feelings that you are having a heart attack, that your head is exploding, or that you are going crazy. You are sure that something is seriously wrong with you and that it is not just nervousness.

3

Frequently these attacks come without warning and appear to be unrelated to anything that is happening.

Albert was watching television when he broke out in a sweat. He felt that everything was unreal, and felt his heart race, pound in his temples, and miss beats. He was sure he was going to collapse and die. He barely managed to get to the telephone to call an ambulance. By the time the examination in the emergency room was completed he felt fine, but he was not convinced that there was nothing physically wrong with him, even though he was told that this was the case. His anxiety was not related to a specific event. He could not predict when the attacks would occur. He had episodes of panic that were much more than normal tension or nervousness. He needed treatment for an anxiety disorder.

Ann is a candidate for a quick fix. Albert can use a quick fix, but needs medical and psychological help as well.

• QUICK FIXES FOR ANXIETY •

DISTRACTION

When you are distracted you are not thinking about yourself. Your mind is on whatever distracted you. Human beings cannot concentrate on more than one thing at a time. Consequently, when you think about something else, you cannot concentrate on your symptoms of anxiety. Your system will calm down and the symptoms will go away.

Ann and Albert both experienced distraction and relief from their anxiety. Ann calmed down after she introduced herself because the ordeal was over and she did not have to think about herself anymore. Albert was distracted by the activity in the emergency room and his anxiety dissipated.

Both Ann and Albert could have used distraction to help themselves before their anxiety became intense and distressing.

If Ann had concentrated on the others in the group, tried to remember their names, or noticed details about them, she would not have developed the tension that made her feel paralyzingly nonfunctional. If Albert had gotten involved in something interesting that took his mind off himself he could have avoided the emergency room. In the hospital he became interested in what

4

the medical staff members were doing and in the test equipment. As his mind focused on other things, the adrenalin stopped coursing through his body and the panic left.

You know best what captivates your mind and distracts you. Use it. You will need to practice whatever distraction you choose because anxiety is a powerful emotion. You can do it. You created the tension because of your thoughts and you can stop it by changing your thoughts. Have several kinds of distractions available so that you have one for every setting. For example, you may not be able to bounce a ball at a party, but you can help the host and hostess. You may not have anyone to talk to at home, but watching television may help you.

——1 · Read

When you are very nervous it is hard to concentrate, so that reading may not be the answer for you. If you do decide that reading can hold your attention pick material that is a real page turner. It probably won't be a self-help book, but it might be a mystery, a horror or an action-packed novel, or something steamy. Select the kind of book that engrosses you. As you lose yourself in the story you will also lose your anxiety.

Barbara found that she could forget her worries and calm down if she turned off the world and tuned into a romance novel. She sat in a special place, put on comfortable clothes, and made it clear to her family that she was on a retreat. She was not to be interrupted. She disconnected the telephone and allowed herself a couple hours of unabashed involvement in the lives of the book's characters. She felt no need to apologize for "wasting time." She found this particularly helpful after a day of pressure from her boss, bad traffic, problems in the family, and guilt feelings about not doing all that she expected of herself.

——2 · Write

When you concentrate on putting words in order you cannot concentrate on your physical tension. Write how you are feeling. Write a letter. Write a story. Write a book telling people how to handle anxiety. Keeping a journal helps with anxiety as this helps you release what is bothering you on a regular basis. When you put your thoughts and worries on paper, you are getting them out of your mind.

Baldwin first used writing to organize his thoughts. He found that was a way to better conceptualize and feel in control of his ideas and plans. This was so effective for him that he started writing down his worries and frustrations. He found that once his concern appeared in written form his anxiety disappeared and his problem-solving skills emerged. Soon he was writing on a daily basis. As he became engaged in writing about his feelings, making lists, and concentrating on recording events, his anxiety subsided. Baldwin found that one-half hour at this activity was all he needed to achieve the desired level of relaxation.

——— 3 · Television

Some people can lose themselves in television. If television is your tranquilizer, use it to relieve your anxiety. Avoid programs that will give you more distress, such as the nightly news. Video-tape programs that engross you or make you laugh. Look at the tapes when your mind needs to be distracted from your physical symptoms of anxiety.

Camille's anxiety inexplicably went away whenever she watched *The Wizard of Oz*. She had her own tape of the film and watched it whenever she felt nervous tension overcome her. She did not know why this helped her. It was enough that it did. She was captivated by the characters and the story. It never failed her. She found that if she watched the tape as soon as the anxiety started she would be ready to resume her normal activity after a few minutes of getting her mind off herself and on to Dorothy and Dorothy's companions.

——— 4 · Projects

A project that requires that you pay attention to what you are doing and includes physical exertion and eye-hand coordination is likely to absorb even the most severe anxiety. Not only are you distracted, but the adrenalin is worked out of your

system through the exercise, and any task that requires eye-hand coordination skills demands all of your attention.

Caesar enjoyed refinishing old furniture. He found that it not only made him feel better, but it enhanced his home environment and his self-esteem. He was the recipient of compliments and praise. However, there was a limit to the amount of refinished furniture he could use in his own household. Consequently, the balm for his anxiety became a way to make extra money as he refinished furniture for others and sold pieces that he found and fixed.

EYE-HAND COORDINATION ACTIVITIES
As indicated in the last quick-fix tip, eye-hand coordination activities are excellent anxiety deescalaters. When the eyes and hands are engaged simultaneously, so is the mind. This is so effective it is a good idea to have antianxiety eye-hand exercise plans for every situation. Some are discreet enough that they can be used in public and when you are surrounded by people.

5 · Games

Games that depend on eye-hand coordination skills come in all sizes and shapes. They can be team sports, such as baseball, soccer, or basketball. They may require at least one other competitor, such as tennis, handball, badminton, shuffleboard, horseshoes, or croquet, or they can be activities that can be done alone such as golf, darts, computer games, or pinball. Games that can surreptitiously occupy you when you are in public and need an eye-hand coordination task to distract you can be purchased at the "dime store." Supply yourself with the hand-held games that are small, lightweight, portable, and enjoin you to shake the steel balls into the small holes to complete the puzzle. Any similar minisized game will do as long as it takes eye-hand coordination performance. Use them while you are on an airplane trip, while a passenger in a car, while standing in line, or even while you are on telephone hold.

Daisy was claustrophobic. This never bothered her overly much as she could generally avoid situations in which she felt closed in. This worked fine until she received her promotion, which included an office on the twentieth floor in the company's building. She found she could not walk this many steps and get to work on time and with the energy to do the job. She had to take the elevator. She solved her problem by buying connect-the-dot books and tearing out a couple of pages at a time which she could conceal in her work portfolio. She diligently worked on these pages during the elevator ride. Not only did she keep her anxiety in check, but she was viewed as a dedicated and industrious employee. Others followed her example and used the elevator ride to plan their daily schedules, make notes, and go over presentations.

Word games such as crossword puzzles also can be used if you fear someone might insist on knowing what you are working on.

———6 · Crafts

Crafts are a great way to use your eye-hand coordination skills. At the same time that you create a finished project you are managing your anxiety.

Crafts come in all sizes and make use of a myriad of materials. Whittling can be done in any place that can accommodate wood shavings. Carving a large wooden statue obviously needs to be carried out in a fixed place. .

Many crafts are highly portable. Knitting, embroidering, crocheting, and needlepoint go anywhere. If the work is automatic and eye-hand coordination is no longer essential, these crafts do not fill the bill.

Painting and drawing are terrific eye-hand coordination activities. If you are not artistic you can still use this approach through the purchase of coloring books or paint-by-number kits.

If you like crafts you will have no trouble finding projects. If you have never tried crafts, go to a hobby or craft store and pick out something that will take concentration and coordination. See if you take to it. If you do not like crafts and the detail work involved makes you nervous, skip to another approach.

Dale could not stand commuting and getting caught in traffic. By the time he got home he was tense and testy. He took to spending one-half hour upon arriving home to work on his model airplane. He emerged from this session in a better mood. His wife and children adapted to this being part of his decompression period that was appreciated by all. To guard against

9

panic attacks engendered by long waits behind backed-up vehicles, Dale pulled out his Lego blocks and worked on them with such interest that he almost regretted getting rolling again.

———7 · Eye-Hand Coordination Exercises

Can you juggle? This may be the time to learn. Bouncing a ball might do it for you. Get a paddle ball and set a new record of consecutive hits. That will keep your mind off yourself and allow your anxiety to disappear voluntarily. Throw pennies into a cup. Braid your daughter's hair. Create your own comforting and challenging eye-hand coordination distraction.

Edie started feeling panicky while having lunch in a restaurant. She tossed butter pats into the ashtray until she calmed down.

———8 · Skills

Do you have special skills that cause you to think and watch what you are doing while you are performing? This might be the case for typists, computer operators, piano players, or cooks. If you can work without watching, this is not for you.

Earl balanced his budget while resolving his restlessness. His tension subsided when he used his adding machine to check expenditures, income, and his bank account.

PEOPLE

People can be a source of anxiety for you, but they are also resources to quiet your anxiety.

———9 · Touch

Human beings orient to touch. Your orientation to touch is stronger than are the responses to stimulation to your senses of taste, smell, sound, and sight. Your tension will crumble when you acknowledge another's touch. Hand-holding or hugging may be enough. Activities that involve more physical contact may be even better. If you suffer debilitating anxiety, support people are important to you. Someone who is trustworthy and available to give you physical comfort is a great asset. However, touch by strangers can help in a pinch. For example:

Faith, like so many who endure anxiety, had a fear of flying. She flew when the job required it, but reluctantly, and with pent-up anxiety. She found that she could ask her seatmate to hold her hand on takeoffs and landings and manage to maintain her equilibrium. So far no one has ever turned her down or objected to her tight grip.

——10 · Talk

Most people have to give some thought to what they say. Even those who seem to speak without thinking have to go through a mental process to select their words. Talking to another person is an effective anxiety reducer. If the talking is purposeful, the effectiveness increases. If you are an anxious person who tends to shrink from social interchange because you feel others will notice that you are not functioning well, or that your anxiety will become totally disabling, change your approach. Get involved. In the first place, people will not notice your problem because they are too busy thinking about themselves. In the second place, you won't notice your problem because you will be too busy thinking about others. Do not be a passive recipient in the social scene. You are to take charge. When you do this you will transcend your anxiety. Use the following procedure.

1. Pick out one person in the crowd.
2. Decide what you want to know about him or her.
3. Interview her or him.
4. When you have the information you want, go to another person, and another, and another.
5. The time will pass rapidly. You will feel success. You will not be distressed by your anxiety.

Fabian dreaded parties. If he went he sat miserably in the corner or pleaded sickness and left. However, he felt he had to go to the farewell party being given for his best friend. He resolved to get through it by using the interviewing technique. He went armed with three questions. They were as follows:

1. What was the interviewee's hobby?

11

2. What was the last book read and/or movie seen?

3. What was the interviewee's favorite vacation?

He promised himself he would follow up each question with more questions, such as why, how, when, tell me more, and who else does it?

Fabian not only conquered his anxiety; he felt himself a social success.

———— 11 · Think of the Other Person

When you think of someone else, you are not thinking of yourself. The truth of the matter is that everyone is self-conscious, looks for approval and acceptance, and craves attention. Keep this in mind. Concentrate on making the other person comfortable and you will become comfortable too. In the process you will make a friend and be regarded as a socially adept person. This will do wonders for your self-esteem. It will help you feel in control!

Gabrielle dreaded the annual office Christmas party. She always felt like a lump. The time spent there seemed an eternity. During one such agonizing event she noticed that the spouses of the employees looked more bored than she felt anxious. She decided to while away some time talking to them. As she worked at helping them have a good time and feel included she started to have a good time herself. She felt powerful when she discovered that her behavior directly influenced others. When she thought about herself it was with confidence, rather than fear. Realizing that other people also have social shyness allowed her to break out of her own problems, make friends, and feel good about herself. An addendum to this happy vignette is that Gabrielle's popularity and social potential increased because those she approached saw her as a pleasant person they wanted to know better. She was invited out more and could polish her skills. This helped her personally and politically.

———— 12 · Help Out

12   Doing nothing is guaranteed to increase your anxiety. The

more you think about your feelings of tension, the more tense you will become. Use people to get yourself out of your self-involvement. At a party, help out. Pass the food and drinks. Empty the ashtrays. If worse comes to worse, do the dishes. You will help yourself by helping others because your mind will shift from your misery to the task at hand. First you will have to think about how to help, then you will have to get busy accomplishing the work. You will be appreciated and you will feel stronger for conquering your anxiety and being able to regulate your own physical and emotional responses.

Gardner could not get out of going to his sister's wedding. It was either attend or face a family fallout. He knew he would hate the wedding and was working himself toward a collapse when his prospective brother-in-law asked him to take charge of the getaway car to make sure it was not decorated or vandalized. Gardner was so vigilant in his task that he forgot to think about his own discomfort. He did his job well, delivered the car unscathed, and learned that he had power over his anxiety.

SUPPORT

Get support. If you are typical of people with anxiety you are ashamed of it. You need not be. Most people will not notice your problem and so won't know to be supportive. Those you tell will be happy to be effective as supports. You can train them to do what you need if you know what you need. What you need is support. This does not mean that you need sympathy, the buck-up approach, or patronizing. You need reassurance, positive suggestions, and triggers. You can also learn to do all of these things for yourself.

—— 13 · Reassurance

Reassurance is a keystone to overcoming anxiety. Until you are able to reassure yourself, train available and important people to do it for you. These people may be family members, friends, or neighbors. It is hoped you will pick people who can be there when you need them.

When you are having an anxiety attack, your response is fear. The fear means that you feel out of control and the fear intensifies. You feel you are going to get worse, embarrass yourself, or even die. You need to know that your attack will not get worse, that your nervous system has memorized a pattern and the worst that can happen has already happened. You will not collapse. You will not die. In fact, the anxiety will go away. You have lived through this before. The attacks have always stopped and they always will. What better reassurance is there? Coach your support person or persons to remind you of the following facts.

1. Nobody notices you are having an attack.
2. You have always gotten over your anxiety attacks before and you will again.
3. The attack will not be worse than anything you have already experienced.
4. You will not collapse or disgrace yourself.
5. You are not dying. You are not sick. You do not have to go to the doctor or the emergency room.
6. You are not going crazy.[1]

Hannah was sure that this was the "big one." Her heart raced. She was seeing double. She was shaking inside and out. She felt as though she was not herself, that there was no meaning to what she was doing, that she was not part of what was going on around her.

Hannah's husband, her designated support person, was away. She was home alone. She wondered if she should call for emergency service since she knew she could not drive herself to the hospital. She was resenting her husband's absence when she started thinking about what he would say if he were there. As she imagined him making reassuring remarks she realized she was pulling herself together. She discerned that she was able to reassure herself. From that day forward her formerly incapacitating anxiety was no longer a serious threat.

———14 · Positive Suggestions

14   It is your negative thoughts that cause your anxiety to intensify.

When you are sure that all is lost, it is hard to be positive. It will help you to be around positive people. It is even more helpful to have someone around who knows how to give you positive suggestions that are within the realm of possibility.

You are suggestible. People who are extremely anxious are. Use the fact that you respond to suggestion to help others help you, and to help yourself. It is your thoughts about yourself and your situation that bring on your anxiety. You are suggesting this dire view of yourself. Change your thoughts and you will change your physical chemistry and the anxiety will leave. If your fears and overwhelming physical responses make it seem an impossible task, recruit someone to do this for you until you are confident enough to do it for yourself.

Some positive suggestions are:
1. I have a strong mind. I brought on the anxiety through my thoughts. I can get rid of the anxiety through my thoughts.
2. I have done well in the past and I can do well now.
3. I am prepared.
4. I am good at this activity.

Whatever your negative concern, coach your support person and yourself to have countervailing positive suggestions. For example:
1. There isn't enough time.
   I can get started and do enough to meet the deadline.
2. He hates me.
   He calls me once a week. That must mean he cares about me.
3. I can't do it.
   I've succeeded before.
4. My decision will be disastrous.
   If the decision is wrong, I can change my mind later.

Halsey was so nervous before every performance that he threw up. He was wretched. The stage manager learned to suggest to him that audiences always gave him a tremendous applause. When Halsey concentrated on this positive outcome instead of his negative fears, his anxiety served to give him a positive edge instead of a pathetic fear.

———15 · Triggers

A trigger is something that brings on or triggers an action or a response. Your trigger has been your tense body or your negative thoughts that bring on increased nervousness and anxiety. What you need is a trigger that brings on relaxation and positive thoughts. Until you can remember to do this for yourself, ask a support person to say the reassuring words.

Your trigger must be individualized. It has to be something to which you relate and respond. It can be a saying, a series of words, or an object.

Some sayings that work are:
—Twenty (or any number you like) years from now it won't make any difference.
—Tomorrow is another day.
—The sun always rises.
—After the dark comes the dawn.
   or even:
—Who cares!

Some object triggers include the following:
—Teddy bears
—TV remote control
—Something of sentimental value
—A book or article that contains information you know to be helpful to you
—Worry beads
—Good luck charms

Ida had an elderly aunt who used to say "Five years from now it won't make any difference." She said it to Ida when she was distraught over an expensive purchase she regretted making. Ida found that that saying allowed her to put the problem in perspective. As she used this trigger her aunt introduced to her she felt immediate relaxation.

———16 · Exercise

Exercise is good for many things and a quick fix for anxiety as well. If you are afraid to exercise because you think it will hurt you, increase your tension, or cause more problems, please understand that you are wrong. Exercise will help you drain off the accumulated adrenalin that builds up in your system when anxiety has set in. Plan to exercise regularly as a preventative measure or as needed to discharge your tension.

You can exercise through work, such as washing the car or the windows.

You can exercise to increase your strength and flexibility through weight lifting or yoga.

You can exercise routinely by walking, running, or bicycle riding.

You can exercise for pleasure and engage in swimming or other sports.

Every time Ian started to exercise he noted that his pulse rate increased. Since he feared a racing heart, exercise increased his anxiety about his physical health. He avoided it. When he finally accepted the assurance that exercise would help, not hurt him, he prospered by walking for one half hour every morning. This gave him a constructive way to start the day, dispelled his early morning tension, and helped him feel confident about his physical and emotional health.

RELAXATION

Relaxation is a good method for reducing tension because muscle fibers lengthen with relaxation and you cannot be tense and relaxed at the same time.

It is not unusual for people to say that trying to relax makes them tense. This does happen. This does not mean that they cannot relax. This means that they need practice. If you are someone who feels a failure at relaxation because you get more unpleasant sensations when you make the effort, do not feel that you have to learn to relax. You can use exercise instead if you are more comfortable with that approach. Pick the quick fixes that work for you! Nevertheless, relaxation is possible for you even if your system seems to react just the opposite way. The truth is that if you can tense your body, you can also relax it. Your mind and mood are making you tense. Your mind and mood can be just as effective in making you relax. You can get so good at relaxation that you can accomplish instant repose.

Besides, there are innumerable relaxation exercises. If one does not do it for you, try another.

———17 · Counting

You have heard the old adage of counting sheep to help you sleep. This is not silly; it works. The reason it works is that your mind and body relax when your concentration is on a boring task. As the sheep are counted the other worries recede because they can't intrude on your awareness when you are engrossed in something else. Counting sheep, or anything else, is not arousing or exciting. You will be calm. You will lose your tension. Count as much and as long as you need to.

In counting, as in all relaxation tasks, your mind will waver from the chosen area of thought. This does not mean that you are failing or that you have imperfect powers of concentration or a short attention span. It is normal. Unbidden and extraneous ideas enter the mind all the time. Gently remind yourself to get back to the exercise you are engaged in and continue your chosen program.

Jacqueline could not sleep because unsolvable problems and fears swirled through her mind. There seemed to be no way to stop them. They went around and around without solution. She was exhausted, but her busy brain kept her awake. She thought that counting sheep was foolish, but she was able to count "pennies from heaven." She saw them falling from the sky and she tallied them as they landed. Each night it took a shorter period of counting for her to relax and drift off to sleep.

———18 · Affirmation Exercise

Stress symptoms occur in the same areas of the body over and over again. When you have anxiety it settles in certain parts of your body every time. These parts of the body become sensitized and become an ongoing problem. The following exercise is designed to reduce your anxiety and relieve the tension in your stressed-out body parts.

1. Sit or lie in a relaxed, comfortable position. Close your eyes.
2. Make a mental trip through your body and concentrate on the areas of tension.
3. As you concentrate on the part of the body that is tense and sore say an affirmation about that part of your physique. For example:
   a. My shoulders feel loose and comfortable.
   b. My neck is supple and pain-free.
   c. My throat is open and able.
   d. My stomach is at ease and functioning well.
   e. My back is relaxed and healthy.
4. As you say the affirmations about your body, visualize that part of your body as healthy and relaxed. For example:
   a. Visualize your shoulders as moving freely.
   b. See your neck as unencumbered and flexible.
   c. Imagine your throat as being able to expand and swallow.
   d. Conceive of your stomach as calm and quiet.
   e. Perceive your back as lithe and strong.

Do this on a regular basis to heal those tender spots that have been assaulted consistently during your tense times.

Jacob always was careful with his neck as it was stiff and hurt when he turned it. This had been a problem for him since his promotion a year ago. He hated his back-biting supervisor who literally gave him a pain in the neck. Jacob felt under pressure at work and nervous about what the administrator would do or say that would make his life difficult. He was feeling anxious and the tension always settled in his neck. He was willing to try anything to feel better (except find another job). He figured he had nothing to lose by doing the affirmation exercise. He did it for ten minutes every morning when he got up, and again in the evening. One month later he noticed that he no longer had neck pain. His pinched nerves and stressed muscles had relaxed enough to relieve the pain. He was so impressed with his success he continued the exercise as a preventive measure.

——19 · Floating

You need relaxation techniques that will work in any environment. Anxiety often occurs in crowds and in public places, or when you are carrying out a responsible function. In these instances you cannot leave, get comfortable, close your eyes, and spend ten minutes in positive and splendid isolation and relaxation. Floating is a quick fix that can be used whenever you need to use it and wherever you are. Floating was popularized by Dr. Claire Weekes who has written excellently and comprehensively about anxiety and phobias.

When using floating, the primary thing you need to tell yourself is that tension is normal; it will not hurt you, and it will go away. The basic first step is acceptance. You accept your anxiety instead of fighting it. It is there. You do not develop more anxiety over the fact that you have anxiety.

The second step is to float. This means that you go with the anxiety. You live through it. You function. You do not panic. You tune into your physical symptoms instead of fighting them. Recognize them and acknowledge them. See them as bodily reactions that will not harm you.

You must also be willing to let time pass for the anxiety to leave, as it always does, and to have a full recovery.

Katherine felt alarm with her first feelings of tension. She feared that any nervousness would proceed into a dreaded panic attack. Her fright, in fact, intensified her anxiety and guaranteed that the anticipated panic attack would occur. This in turn made her sure that simple tension could not ever come and go without frightful results. She was in a discouraging fear-panic spiral. She felt she had nothing to lose if she tried floating. Acceptance was hard for her as she knew that she would feel terrible before she felt better. But as she practiced acceptance, and concentrated on getting through, instead of fighting off the anxiety, her symptoms became less painful and she experienced success. She developed confidence through floating through her anxiety, taking the time to recover, and overcoming her fear. She learned that she would not have to have recurring panic attacks.

Breathing is something you do continually and something you
hope to continue doing automatically.

——20 · Deep Breathing

When you are under stress your breathing becomes more rapid
and shallow. You can interrupt this pattern anytime, anywhere,
by taking a few deep breaths.

Deep breathing is an effective quick fix for tension. You can
do this when you are in church, or on an airplane, or when you
are talking with your boss. Other breathing exercises are also
of use.

——21 · Square Breathing

Square breathing is a form of deep breathing, but is more powerful.

1. Breathe in and hold your breath for a count of four.
2. Breathe out as you count to four.
3. Hold your breath to the count of four.
4. Breathe in as you count to four.
5. Repeat steps one to four as often as necessary.

If counting to four does not work for you, try to count to
three or five. Just use the same count for the breath holding
and the breathing in and breathing out.

Kane engaged in deep breathing almost automatically as it
kept his tension at bay. Physical sensations that indicated anxiety
were his trigger to deep breathe. He could use the technique
unself-consciously for short intervals until the nervousness was
under control. When he felt particular stress before an important business or social engagement he used square breathing. By doing this he managed more severe pangs of panic. He
achieved more control with square breathing because it was less
automatic and took more concentration since he had to count
while he was breathing. Like deep breathing, it kept him from
dizziness, shortness of breath, chest pain, shaking, nausea, and

confusion because it reduced the production of carbon dioxide that occurred when Kane allowed the anxiety to go unchecked while he took short, shallow breaths.

——22 · Quickie

Any quick-fix book should have a quickie exercise. This terrific breathing exercise is it! The quickie takes only a few seconds and can be used anywhere and as often as needed. It is particularly good in an emergency as it not only reduces tension, but suggests to you that you are ready to handle the situation.

1. Say to yourself "Alert mind, calm body."
2. Smile. You may have to smile inwardly if a smile would be inappropriate in the circumstances. The smile interrupts the fixed jaw and clenched teeth of tense times. Think grin, not grim.
3. Let your shoulders and arms sag. Tension often concentrates in the shoulders. The sag gives the feeling of the tension running down your arms and out of your body.
4. Take a deep breath.
5. Continue your normal activity.

If you have to do this fifty or sixty times a day, do not despair. Each time it is a quick fix. As you continuously succeed you are developing new patterns that will lead to the long-range permanent fix.

——23 · Rhythmic Breathing

Rhythmic breathing is the basis of all relaxation exercises. When you learn to breathe using the muscles of the abdomen, you are well on the way to being able to benefit from a relaxation regimen. When you learn rhythmic breathing you are training your muscles, your reflexes, and your mind. You are in charge. No longer are you at the total mercy of your autonomic nervous system. You can do what you need and want to do to maintain your physical well-being.

To teach yourself rhythmic breathing:

1. Get comfortable. You may sit or stand, but close your eyes and place the palms of your hands on your stomach.
2. Breathe in through your nostrils to the count of four. Feel your stomach expand.
3. Exhale through your mouth to a slow count of four. Feel the air leave your stomach.
4. Repeat as needed or as time allows.

Lacey used the quickie in traffic. It kept her anxiety and temper in check. She went home in a better mood. But sometimes the stress of work, the commute, and demands on her once she hit the door of her house were more than she thought she could manage. She learned rhythmic breathing and did it at each traffic light. By the time she arrived home she had reoriented herself and was ready for whatever awaited her.

———24 · Affirmative Breathing

Affirmative breathing quiets the body and the mind. It can be used to respond to triggers of fear and self-doubts. When you are having negative thoughts, take a breath and switch to a positive thought. This instant exercise brings immediate relief.

Lamar was shaking. He had to finish a report for the office, mow the lawn before his in-laws arrived, take his daughter to Little League, and feed the dog. He was thinking that he couldn't do it all. He took a breath, said to himself, "I can do what I can do," and relaxed. Whenever the pressures and shakes started he repeated the exercise. He soon found that he could change any negative into a positive. For him this was a signal to relax. He used affirmative breathing when his luggage was lost (It is one thing less to carry), and when his septic tank overflowed (Someone else can fix this). He became a person who responded to problems rather than reacted to them.

———25 · Calm Breathing

Calm breathing incorporates and enhances rhythmic breathing. It integrates the body and the mind.

1. Close your eyes. Press one nostril closed with your thumb. Fill your abdomen and lungs with an intake of air. Think of this air as going to your forehead. Imagine the air is tinted a calming shade of blue. See the color filling your body while bringing health and harmony to your entire being.
2. Release your thumb and hold your opposite nostril closed with your finger. Hold your breath for up to ten counts. See the air you inhaled collecting all your fears and worries. Exhale, expelling all your tensions with your breath.
3. Repeat as needed.

——26 · Restful Breathing

Many breathing exercises are so restful that they are ideal to help you wind down before retiring for the night. They not only treat your anxiety but also are a remedy for your sleeplessness.

1. Lie on your back on the floor with your arms along your sides. Close your eyes.
2. As you breathe in, raise your arms slowly up and over your head to a comfortable count of ten.
3. Reverse the procedure slowly, bringing your arms down to your side while you count to ten.

If ten seems too long for you, start with a lower number and work up to ten.

4. Repeat this exercise ten times as you fall into a trancelike state.

SPECIFIC TECHNIQUES FOR RELAXING

When you relax your muscles you also relax your nervous system. Your muscles and nerves work as a unit. Your nerves cannot stay tense when your muscles are relaxed. To make sure that you find a way to relax your muscles, a buffet of relaxation models are presented for your experimentation and choice. Different drills are suggested for different people.

—27 · Body Rejuvenation

This quick fix can be practiced over an eight week period. Gather four small pillows. Go to bed and get comfortable in the following way.

1. Place one pillow under your head and neck. Place one pillow under your knees. Place a pillow on each side of your chest. Lay your arms on them with your hands hanging over the edge.
2. Close your eyes.
3. Talk silently to your jaw saying, "Let go, let go." Say, "Let go more, let go more."
4. Do this thirty minutes daily for one week.
5. The second week relax your jaw as usual and concentrate on your arms.
6. Talk silently to your arms saying, "Arms let go, let go." Say, "Let go more, let go more."

25

7. The third week relax your jaw and arms as usual and concentrate on your chest.
8. Talk silently to your chest saying, "Chest let go, let go." Say, "Let go more, let go more."
9. The fourth week relax your jaw, arms, and chest as usual and concentrate on your legs.
10. Talk silently to your legs saying, "Legs let go, let go." Say, "Let go more, let go more."
11. The fifth week relax your jaw, arms, chest, and legs as usual and concentrate on your back.
12. Talk silently to your back saying, "Back, let go, let go." Say, "Let go more, let go more."
13. The sixth week relax your jaw, arms, chest, legs, and back as usual and concentrate on your neck.
14. Talk silently to your neck saying, "Neck, let go, let go." Say, "Let go more, let go more."
15. The seventh week relax the jaw, arms, chest, legs, and neck as usual and concentrate on your face.
16. Talk silently to your face saying, "Face, let go, let go." Say, "Let go more, let go more."
17. The eighth week relax your jaw, arms, chest, legs, neck, and face as usual and concentrate on your scalp.
18. Talk silently to your scalp saying, "Scalp let go, let go." Say, "Let go more, let go more."

Always talk to yourself while doing this relaxation exercise as it shortens the learning time.

Once your muscles and nervous system have memorized the feeling of relaxation you will be able to relax in social situations and during other tense moments, such as in the dentist's chair (well, maybe) by saying, "Let go, let go." to yourself.

Maude applied herself diligently and spent eight weeks learning this form of progressive relaxation. When she was three weeks into the exercise she was struck by how much better her arms felt in comparison to other parts of her body. In the end she added a ninth and tenth week to give special concentration to her stomach and her eye muscles. She continued the exercise daily, and could relax in an instant because of her self-training. She continued to put in thirty minutes a day to enjoy her skill, rest her muscles and nerves, and clear her mind. She found she could quickly and easily relax at her desk, and on the bus, and while she was visiting her accountant. She knew she was physically and mentally healthier.

28 · Autosuggestion

You talk to yourself all the time. Most of your talk is negative and creates tension. Relaxation exercises require that you talk to yourself in a positive way that allows relaxation. You suggest to yourself that you are comfortable and calm. This is called autosuggestion.

Get comfortable and concentrate on breathing rhythmically (see the section on Rhythmic Breathing). Then start your auto-suggestions. Continue them for ten minutes.

My neck feels heavy, warm, and relaxed.
My neck feels heavy, warm, and relaxed.

My shoulders feel heavy, warm, and relaxed.
My shoulders feel heavy, warm, and relaxed.

My arms feel heavy, warm, and relaxed.
My arms feel heavy, warm, and relaxed.

My back feels heavy, warm, and relaxed.
My back feels heavy, warm, and relaxed.

My legs feel heavy, warm, and relaxed.
My legs feel heavy, warm, and relaxed.

My whole body feels heavy, warm, and relaxed.
My whole body feels heavy, warm, and relaxed.

My mind is quiet and still.
I am relaxing more and more deeply.
I am relaxing more and more deeply.

My mind is quiet and still.
I am relaxing more and more deeply.
I am relaxing more and more deeply.[2]

27

Madison suffered from test anxiety. His grades reflected his inability to concentrate. He complained that his mind went blank whenever he took a test. Madison worked at autosuggestion until he found he could relax whenever he wanted to. He then added the following suggestions to help himself at test taking time.

I can remember everything I learned.

I can concentrate on each question.

I am confident and relaxed and will get a good grade.

You know the happy ending to this story. Madison corrected his negative self-talk, started succeeding in test taking, developed confidence, and no longer had test anxiety. If he did feel tense he was able to relax and suggest positive results to himself.

────29 • "The Releaxation Response"

No quick-fix book would be complete without Dr. Herbert Benson's relaxation response.[3] He based his techniques on transcendental meditation, which is a good relaxation method, but not a quick fix. Actually, by now you are aware that relaxation is not a quick fix unless you first learn the method. Once learned, you will be able to relax immediately. You will realize it is well worth the investment of the time it takes to develop your skill.

The relaxation response, like other relaxation routines, will help lower your blood pressure, slow your heartbeat, and inhibit your gastric acid secretions. This happens because the mental centering hushes mental activity and quiets the bodily reactions.

1. Sit comfortably in a quiet place where you will not be disturbed. Dr. Benson recommends thirty minutes for optimum benefit.
2. Close your eyes and let your mind wander for about one minute.
3. Choose a word that is a relaxing word to you, or a word that has no meaning to you, or a neutral number.
4. Repeat this word or number to yourself for the next twenty minutes. As your mind wanders from the word or number, as it will, simply be aware that this is happening, and return to saying the word or number to yourself.
5. When you feel that about thirty minutes have passed,

peek at a clock and gradually emerge from your relaxed state.

A variation on this includes focusing on a neutral object such as a candle, a paper clip, a sphere, or anything that does not conjure up emotion. Think about its size, shape, color, and texture and as your thoughts distract you, gently return your focus to the object. This can be used instead of closing your eyes and thinking of a word or number.

Another variation is the use of a timer. Dr. Benson recommends against this, but some people need to know that the time allotted is being automatically counted. This is the only way they can free their minds to engage in the relaxation response.

Nadine ignored Dr. Benson's recommendation that the relaxation response be practiced two times a day. She felt lucky to be able to manage it once daily. Even at that she varied it to suit her needs. She allowed herself twenty minutes. She sat in a quiet place. She concentrated on her throat. She imagined it tense, relaxed, swallowing, open, closed, and sore, and always ended up saying that her throat was relaxed, healthy, and functioning well. She combined autosuggestion and the mental centering of the relaxation response to relax the one area of her body that gave her the most trouble. Before she did this she had trouble talking and eating when she was tense. She felt it was a problem that was beyond her control. Through a tailor-made relaxation program she discovered that her throat problem was a transitory difficulty that responded to a quick fix. After she perfected her skill she only had to say, "functioning well" to herself. This triggered relaxation and a throat that performed perfectly.

——— 30 · Autogenics[4]

You may not get instant results with autogenics, but it takes very little time per day to work the autogenics program. And while you are experiencing this exercise you are incrementally getting benefits. It is a relaxation technique that requires you to devote several minutes, several times a day in passive concentration. You can increase the time spent on the exercise, or work out any time combination that suits you. As reported here, autogenics is a twelve-week program to master.

As always, get comfortable in a quiet place and close your eyes.

Week one
Heaviness theme
Take about five seconds to say this group of statements, pause for about three seconds, and repeat it about four times.
My right arm is heavy.
My left arm is heavy.
Both of my arms are heavy.
At the end say, When I open my eyes I will feel fresh and alert.

Week two
Increase your time and repetitions.
My right arm is heavy.
My left arm is heavy.
Both of my arms are heavy.
My right leg is heavy.
My left leg is heavy.
Both of my legs are heavy.
My arms and legs are heavy.
When you are through say, When I open my eyes I will feel fresh and alert.

Week three
Increase your time and repetitions over what you did during week two.
My right arm is heavy.
Both of my arms are heavy.
Both of my legs are heavy.
My arms and legs are heavy.
In closing say, When I open my eyes I will feel fresh and alert.

Week four
Warmth theme
Continue to increase your time and repetitions.
My right arm is heavy.

My arms and legs are heavy.
My right arm is warm.
My left arm is warm.
Both of my arms are warm.
Include at the end, When I open my eyes I will feel fresh and alert.

Week five
If you can continue to increase your time and repetitions, do so.
My right arm is heavy.
My arms and legs are heavy.
My right arm is warm.
My left arm is warm.
My left leg is warm.
Both of my legs are warm.
My warms and legs are warm.
Always end with, When I open my eyes I will feel fresh and alert.

Week six
By now you may have increased your time to ten minutes, three times a day.
My right arm is heavy.
My arms and legs are heavy.
Both of my arms are warm.
Both of my legs are warm.
My arms and legs are warm.
My arms and legs are heavy and warm.
In closing say, When I open my eyes I will feel fresh and alert.

Week seven
Continue as in week six, increasing time and repetitions slightly if you want to.
My right arm is heavy.
My arms and legs are heavy.
My arms and legs are warm.
My arms and legs are heavy and warm.
Before stopping say, When I open my eyes I will feel fresh and alert.

Week eight
Hearbeat theme
Move at your own pace, increasing time and repetitions so that the exercise does not interfere with your schedule, but gets included several times a day.
My right arm is heavy.
My arms and legs are heavy and warm.
My heartbeat is calm and regular.
Never quit without saying, When I open my eyes I will feel fresh and alert.

Week nine
Breathing theme
Increases in time and repetitions should level off to a comfortable amount of time that seems right for you.
My right arm is heavy.
My arms and legs are heavy and warm.
My heartbeat is calm and regular.
It breathes me.
Remember to say, When I open my eyes I will feel fresh and alert.

Week ten
Solar plexus theme
My right arm is heavy.
My arms and legs are heavy and warm.
My heartbeat is calm and regular.
It breathes me.
My solar plexus is warm.
End with, When I open my eyes I will feel fresh and alert.

Week eleven
Forehead theme
My right arm is heavy.
My arms and legs are heavy and warm.
My heartbeat is calm and regular.
It breathes me.
My solar plexus is warm.
My forehead is cool.
Last words are, When I open my eyes I will feel fresh and alert.

Week twelve
Special themes
Add any suggestions that have meaning to you, such as:
My mind is quiet.
I am at ease.
I feel secure.
Or address special problems, such as:
There is nothing wrong with me.
I am healthy.
I am an attractive person.
People like me.
I am a confident person, secure in any situation.
Always add, When I open my eyes I will feel fresh and alert.

Include anything you want as long as it is brief, believable, and affirming. Remember, this is passive concentration. If your mind wanders, let it. Keep saying the lines repetitively and your mind will wander back.

Napoleon liked the progressive nature of this relaxation exercise as he felt he could get used to it and slowly work it into his routine. But he could not respond to the verbal suggestions. He solved this by visualizing heavy weights pulling on his arms and legs, sunshine beating on his warm body, and a cool cloth on his forehead.

———31 · Biofeedback

Biofeedback is a technique for measuring your tension and taking your temperature. In this way it is not much different than a thermometer. A blood pressure machine is another example of a biofeedback machine in that it tells you what is happening in your body.

A biofeedback machine works because tension increases the blood flow to the long muscles in the legs and arms and away from the extremities, the fingers and toes. As the blood leaves these areas they become cooler. Cold extremities mean tension. The temperature gauge on the biofeedback machine drops and a buzzer sounds, indicating an emotional change. Biofeedback is a clear indication of how your mood affects the body. Think-

33

ing about unpleasant, stressful events will set off the buzzer as your involuntary nervous system responds immediately to your thoughts. You can change the autonomic system by changing your thoughts. You can learn to do this by using biofeedback. You can get biofeedback training from anyone who has a machine and is licensed to conduct this therapy. You learn what makes you tense and how to relax. Relaxation causes the blood to flow back to your hands and feet. Consequently, they will warm up. The buzzer will stop. The most remarkable lesson is how quickly your state of mind affects your body. You can perform biofeedback in the comfort of your own home by placing your hand on a sheet of white paper and imagining your hand getting darker in color. This concentration will reverse your tension. You will observe the results. Your nerves will be calm and the blood will move back into your extremities. Visualization can work as well. Picture your hand in hot water, over an open fire, or on a heating pad. These thoughts will actually warm your hand and relax your body.

Odelia, a psychiatrist, got more tense the first time she tried biofeedback. She felt a failure personally and professionally. She wanted to reduce her tension, but thought if she couldn't do the exercise as directed, she must be out of control. If she could not help herself, how could she help others?

What Odelia did not know was that the pressure to perform made her more tense so that her fingers got colder and paler. The fact that her mind had such an impact on her body showed that she had the power, could manage the technique, and had only to change her thoughts. When this was explained, she tried again and imagined flames leaping from her fingers. Warmth and blood returned to her extremities within fifteen minutes. She felt in control of her bodily reactions and no longer at the inexplicable mercy of her anxiety.

———32 · Inner Peace

Relaxation is good to learn because of the immediate relief you feel after you have mastered it and can relax your body at will. It is also good because it gives you mind over matter. Your mind has domination over your body.

The inner peace relaxation techniques are based on Dr. Norman Vincent Peale's think positive techniques.

1. Close your eyes.
2. Say to yourself: My mind is free of worry, bitterness, distress, and frustration. Visualize them all leaving. Give them shapes or colors so that you can see them drain, tumble, or march out of your head.
3. Say to yourself: My mind is full of kindness, confidence, ability, and peace. Imagine each one entering your brain and getting comfortable in your mind.
4. Take two or three deep breaths.
5. Think of peaceful scenes while you relax your facial muscles.
6. Think tranquillity and serenity.
7. Carry on with your normal occupations.

Ogden was ready to call off his first date with the girl of his dreams. All he could think of was failure, rejection, and his awkwardness. All day before the date (after he was persuaded to go through with it) he regularly worked on his inner peace. He was not without tension when he picked up his date, but it was not a painful attack of nerves. It was just enough tension to give him a feeling of excitement and anticipation. Since he had implanted the ideas of peace, ability, and confidence in his mind the mild tension felt good, like the introduction to a pleasurable experience. This is an excellent example to illustrate that you are what you think you are. Don't you just love happy endings?

——33 · Visualization

Visualization means that you focus your awareness by seeing your tension as a color, a shape, or an image. Visualization is helpful for getting rid of tension in specific places in your body, for ridding yourself of pain, and for managing stress.

Start visualization by closing your eyes. Be aware of the tension areas in your body. Give these body areas symbols such as ice, red, or fire. Now picture relaxation as the sun, blue, or cool water. Picture the sun melting the ice, blue lights flashing on to replace the red, or cool water putting out the fire. Feel yourself relax as this occurs.

Pamela's anxiety always settled in her chest. She felt her heart would explode when she got anxious. She visualized her chest with an iron band around it. Relaxation was symbolized as a leprechaun with a laser beam that could cut through the metal and release her. As she imagined her chest being released she felt comfort come to her body.

────34 · Guided Imagery

Tape your own guided imagery trip on a tape recorder so you can listen to your own voice. Your guided imagery can be customized with places and symbols that are useful to you. Be sure to include the following elements:

1. A relaxing environment with pleasant sights, sounds, and smells.
2. A place to which you can imagine yourself walking and then settling in.

For example:

Get comfortable and close your eyes. See yourself leaving the area in which you live and walking across a long, warm beach. You are leaving all your hassles and pressures behind. You are getting closer to the water. You wade in and it is cool and soothing. As you walk back across the sand you come upon a stand of trees creating a pleasant environment of sun and shade. You walk down a path and find a comfortable place to stop. You look at what is bothering you. You give your worries shapes and colors and examine them closely. After scrutinizing them you put them down along the path and continue up a low hill. You look around and find an inviting, comfortable place. You memorize how this place looks, feels, smells, and sounds. You settle in and relax. You look around again and know that this is your special place to relax and to which you can go anytime you want. As you leave your place of special relaxation tell yourself that this is your own place you have created and that you can use whenever you want to relax.

Palmer probably hated cocktail parties more than anything. He never knew what to do or say and was tense and self-conscious until he could get away. He tried to avoid them but now and then he would go because his wife insisted that it was important. After Palmer had practiced guided imagery to a mountain stream and made this imaginary place his own personal retreat, he could manage the events much better. Whenever he felt tense he would see himself happy, content, and relaxed in his sylvan setting. He could smell the fresh air and feel the cool breeze. The few seconds it took for him to do this changed his mood and he could go and greet another person and engage in another round of small talk.

35 · Structured Review

Sometimes you are in a bad mood because of something that happened, but you aren't sure what it is. Because you don't know what it is you can't let it go. Structured review is a relaxation exercise that will help you remember and let go. You can start the exercise at any time of the day and do it anywhere, anytime. It is especially good at bedtime as a technique for letting go of the day's accumulated experiences and attendant feelings.

Think of the start of your day. Who was there? What were you doing? What were your thoughts? How did you feel? Let it go. It is past. You cannot change it now.

Move to the rest of your morning. What was it like? Who was there? What were you doing? What were your thoughts? How did you feel? Let it go. It is past. You cannot change it now.

Go through your entire day in this manner, stopping or starting whenever you need or want. At the end tell yourself that you are in the present, the now, and that you are relaxed.

Quentin was in his car one noon, riding along and feeling poorly. He wasn't sure why, but he felt anxious, irritable, and unhappy. He used the structured review exercise to go over his morning and recognized that he was uneasy about an investment he made at the bank. He knew that what he had done could not be changed until six months had passed. He told himself it was past. It couldn't be changed. Let it go. He did. His mood brightened. He relaxed.

36 · Music

Music is relaxing for many. It can cheer people up and calm people down. Music can be part of any relaxation program or a certain piece of music can trigger relaxed feelings for you.

Be careful in your selection. You want soothing, not depressing music, cheerful, not hyper music.

Rachel was depressed and anxious about her breakup with her boyfriend. Some days she did not think she could stand it. She noticed that when she was in her car she felt worse than at any other time. One day a friend riding with her remarked on the mournful sound of the music she was playing on her tape player. She then realized that she was contributing to her own unhappiness and tension with the music she had selected. She picked some tunes that were a little more cheerful than she felt, but were still tranquil. The upbeat music she played elevated her mood and stilled her anxiety.

Helpful Techniques

The following helpful hints may sound off-the-wall. I can assure you that they have aided people whose anxiety has ranged from mild tension to panic attacks. They are quick fixes that abate the anxious feelings while they are occurring.

37 · Imagine that another person is with you when you feel you might get out of control, such as when you are shopping in a supermarket, standing in line, or driving a car.

38 · Read reassuring articles and sayings that you believe and that reinforce the idea that you are healthy and will continue that way.

39 · Focus on one thing. For example, when you are in an airplane look at something on the ground or any other fixed object. When you are standing in line concentrate on the cashier.

40 · Wear earplugs while you are flying so airplane noises do not alarm you.

41 · Sit down and lift your legs in the air.

42 · Drink water.

43 · Use cold compresses.

44 · Chew gum.

45 · Use a hot water bottle.

46 · Hold ice to your neck.

47 · Pet the cat or dog.

48 · Write: I am safe. Write it as many times as you need to.

49 · Run around the block.

50 · Have your support person write a guarantee that you will not fall apart and embarrass yourself, that you are not going crazy, that you won't die, that it won't get any worse, and that the anxiety will pass. Keep this with you to refer to as needed.

51 · Get out your medical report to reassure yourself that you are healthy.

39

——52 · Telephone someone.

——53 · Leave the situation that makes you anxious.

——54 · Have a prewritten plan for handling anxious times. Consult it as needed and follow the plan.

——55 · Remind yourself that tension is a normal, not dangerous, bodily response to tense situations and thoughts.

——56 · Do not take your pulse. If you feel you must, tell yourself that your heart is working well.

——57 · Know the smells that soothe you and have that smell on hand to calm you when it is needed. Cypress emits a tranquil scent.

——58 · Stand back from a wall, lean into it, placing your hands flat against it. Push against the wall. This controls nervousness and releases energy.

——59 · Hiss, stretching out the ssssss. Push your palms flat together in front of you, fingers pointing up. Relax and inhale.

——60 · Count the money you have on hand.

61 · Make a list of:
—all the people you know
—the states you have visited
—baseball players you remember
—chores to do
—places you would like to go

62 · Listen to a talk show on the radio or a tape that captures your attention or gives you reassurance.

63 · Look at four or five objects and try to remember details about all of them.

64 · Organize your purse or your wallet.

65 · Breathe into a paper bag.

66 · Massage one side of your neck. The carotid artery is at the angle of the jaw and the neck, in front of and just below the ear. Massaging this artery will slow your heart rate. Do not massage both sides as that could cut off the blood supply to your brain.

67 · Concentrate on all the sounds in your environment. How many can you hear? What are they?

68 · Repeat, "There is nothing here to

make me afraid. I am doing this to myself and I can undo it."

69 · Eat something you really love and tell yourself all the reasons you think it is so great to consume.

70 · Get uncomfortable. Wearing tight clothes, or pinching shoes, or sitting or standing in an unnatural position will be annoying as well as painful. You will be distracted from your anxiety because you will orient to your discomfort.

71 · Stay uncomfortable. Walk around on gravel. You will soon forget your anxiety because you will be thinking about your sore feet.

72 · See how many times you can multiply 3 times 6 before it totals 1,000.

73 · Health Habits

Although good health habits are cumulative and generally help only over time, certain health habits are quick fixes for those of you who struggle with anxiety. These are:

Do not smoke or use tobacco. The nicotine is a stimulant to the nervous system.

Do not use caffeine in any form. Do not drink coffee, tea, colas, or chocolate. Caffeine increases the pulse rate and thus causes discomfort for those of you who tune into what your body is doing.

Do not drink alcohol. The rebound effect from alcohol will be alarming to you if you are an anxious person.

Eat regularly even if you do not feel like it. When your body is fueled it will feel better. Feeling better makes you more relaxed about yourself.

Rest as needed. Pushing yourself beyond your endurance will give you physical stress, which you don't need.

For further help see Chapter 3 Stress, Chapter 2 Worry, and Chapter 4 Shyness.

• NOTES •

1. Claire Weekes, *Hope and Help for Your Nerves.* (New York: Bantam Books, 1969).
2. Barbara Dossey, "A Wonderful Prerequisite," *Nursing 84* (January 1984): 42–45.
3. Herbert Benson, and Merian Z. Klipper, *The Relaxation Response* (New York: Avon, 1975).
4. Luthe Wolfgang, "Autogenic Training: Method, Research, and Application in Medicine," *American Journal of Psychotherapy* (1963): 194–95.

Chapter TWO

WORRY

YOU MAY BE PROUD you are a worrier. You may feel that it is your responsibility to worry. Further, you may think that your worrying has prevented many disasters. If this is your belief you will have a hard time giving up worrying. But even if you cannot give it up, you can handle your worries in a more constructive way.

You may be able to manage your worry by channeling it into problem solving. Others of you who feel the obligation to worry can control it by using techniques that will help you regulate it.

• SYMPTOMS •

Everyone worries. It is how you worry that makes the difference. Worrying with no purpose wastes energy, causes the body to tense, gives you a feeling of helplessness, and disrupts your life. Often the chronic worrier complains of problems with insomnia and concentration and feels generally below par. Worrying constricts the enjoyment of life and keeps you from taking effective action.

According to Dr. Wayne W. Dyer, author of *Your Erroneous Zones,* worriers are dependent on their worries to keep themselves from dealing with problems.[1] The worrier avoids the present problems by brooding over uncontrollable problems, using worry to postpone action and worrying about someone else in order to be seen as a caring person.

Ralph was your garden-variety worrier. He worried more than he wanted to. Sometimes worrying kept him awake at night. Now and then his worrying interfered with his ability to have fun. He did not like it. He wanted to change. A quick fix could work for him.

Sabina was practically nonfunctional because of her worries. She worried about her health, the health of everyone she knew, her finances, the finances of everyone she knew, her children, the state of the lawn, the car, the cat, the environment, and the world. Because of her worries she was always cautious, never spontaneous. She had problems experiencing happiness and spent most of her time warding off anticipated catastrophes. A quick fix could help Sabina develop some control over her worries, but professional help is indicated to achieve a cure.

• HOW TO WORRY BETTER •
• DIFFERENT AND LESS •

———74 • Let It Simmer

Work at developing a let it simmer approach to problems. Many problems solve themselves. Other problems should be managed by the people to whom the problems belong. Some turn out not to be problems at all. If you can wait, more options for handling the problem often present themselves.

Once you have experimented with this approach, you will develop confidence in it. You will be amazed and thrilled with the way things really do work out without your assistance.

Salvatore was an executive who believed in solving problems as they came up. If a contract wasn't signed, he barged ahead. An employee having problems was a signal for a behavior counseling conference. If something broke, he fixed it. One Friday he discovered that one of his most valued employees was planning to quit and there were bad feelings among the contenders for the position. Normally he would put his entire being into worrying about this problem until he figured out the best way to handle it. He would then take quick action. In the meantime he was unapproachable. He could not think about anything else and was short tempered because he had "things on his mind."

However, he could not devote himself entirely to the situation because his daughter had been in a car accident (She was not hurt) and she needed transportation to go to the college she attended. He was taken up with that worry, as well as with the damaged car, the insurance, the police report, and his daughter's well-being, so he couldn't concentrate on the problem of his ambitious staff members. By the time he was able to stop worrying about his daughter and start worrying about the business he learned that an awaited reorganization was about to take place. The favored employee was appointed as his second in command. He did not leave. Those vying for his job were suited for the department head positions that had opened up.

Salvatore learned something from this. Not everything required his intense worrying or aggressive handling. When he heard his daughter was leaving college to marry an unemployed poet he let it simmer. Even though the romance flourished Salvatore kept his worrying in check. When the poet left to live in India, Salvatore was relieved. This reinforced his let it simmer theory and kept him from worrying steadily and rushing in rapidly. You may have used this approach when you said, "I'll sleep on it," or "Things will look better tomorrow."

———75 · Question Worry's Effectiveness

1. Ask how worrying will help the situation.

    Tab worried about getting old. He watched old people to see how they looked and acted. He noticed every twinge and wrinkle in his own body. Tab had to realize that worrying was not keeping him from aging, but it was keeping him from enjoying the present as much as he could.

2. Ask what is the worst that can happen.

    Tamara always worried about her schedule. She started out tense every morning, feeling rushed before she kept her first appointment or tackled her first job. When she asked herself what was the worst thing that could happen she realized that being late or missing a meeting would not be crucial in the long run. Besides, she had seldom been late in the five years she had held the job.

3. Ask if you are worrying in order to avoid something.

    Ulla had pains in her chest. She worried about them for

two months before she had to go to the doctor for another problem. She mentioned the pains to her doctor and learned that her heart was not in danger. She took medicine and was fine. While she worried about her chest pains, she was able to avoid physical activities she did not enjoy.

Udell worried that his book would not be accepted by any publisher, so he put off writing it.

4. Ask if worrying will change anything.

Valentina spent every summer worrying about hurricanes. Her worrying did not prevent their occurrence.

Wanda worried about her son getting into the school of his choice. He didn't, but he got a college degree and went into work he enjoyed. Worrying did not make something happen, or make it better or worse.

———76 · Put It Off

When you see worrying as a choice, you can manage it better. You can decide when it is convenient to worry. If you feel a worry attack coming on, postpone it. Tell yourself you do not have time or do not want to worry about it now and delay it. Put off the worry for ten minutes. When the ten minutes are up you can defer for another ten minutes if you decide you want to.

Val had to speak at a convention and was very worried about it. Her worries put her into a state of being unable to prepare her presentation because everything she thought of saying did not seem good enough. As the deadline approached, her worries intensified. Motivated by necessity she tried worry postponement. She said to herself, "I'll do this first and worry about it a half hour after I get a good start." She applied herself diligently, got into her project, and when the half hour was up she again put off her appointment with worry. After she was finished with her plan for her presentation she told herself she could worry. By that time she no longer needed to.

———77 · Let Someone Else Do the Worrying

If someone else is worrying about the same thing, person, or event as you are, isn't that enough? This is a case in which two heads are not better than one. Be energy efficient. Don't double the effort. Let the other person or persons take on the job of worrying.

Wade was a world-class worrier. He worried about taxes, about the way the city was run, if the rug needed vacuuming, and if the cat stayed out too late. He always felt his wife did not understand the seriousness of the problem because she did not fret, fume, and find herself unable to concentrate on anything else because of the worry at hand. Her philosophy was that it was not necessary for her to worry as Wade did enough worrying for two people. In spite of his aggravation with her, his wife refused to worry. She let him add his worry that she did not worry enough to his long list of problems with which he burdened his brain.

Results of research on medical patients indicate that people who do not worry fare better after surgery. Those who turned their worries over to the people who were caring for them had fewer complications after surgery. There were fewer incidences of nausea, fever, headache, and infection. These patients left the hospital sooner.[2]

Coronary patients were studied by Dr. Thomas P. Hackett, who found that those who were calm and fatalistic more often survived than those who worried constantly. The worrier does not know when to stop. The nonworrier learns what needs to be learned, then turns the problem over to the experts and lets them worry about it. Isn't this why you hire physicians, accountants, mechanics, and housekeepers? They are employed because of what they know how to do and because they can take care of the problem. If you cannot trust the person you hire, hire someone you can.

——78 · Get Busy

Worthwile work wards off worry. When you spend time in endeavors you enjoy you will worry less. If you feel the work you are doing makes a contribution to the well-being of people and places you care about, your worries will become less pronounced.

Xena worked off her worries in her garden. When she emerged she felt happy with her neatly weeded rows of vegetables and flowers. Instead of distress she felt accomplishment. Whatever was worrying her was not important anymore. She had taken purposeful, meaningful time off from her concerns. In distancing herself she gained a better perspective.

Jennifer found that action expelled her worries. She took action related to her worry. If she found herself worried about termites she had her house inspected. If she was brooding over work problems she talked to her administrator. If she was moping about anything she could do something about she did that something rather than chafe.

——79 · Learn from It

Think about it instead of worrying about it. Is it past? Can you do anything about it? Let it go. Write it off. But don't let it be a complete wipeout. You can learn from it. Analyze what happened and why. Extract what knowledge you can from the experience.

Xavier gave a dinner party. He planned it to the last detail, worrying all the time. At the last minute two of the six guests canceled and two arrived late. The other two were on a diet and couldn't eat all that he served. Then the cat jumped into the middle of the table and made a lunge for the roast beef. With this Xavier felt all his worry had been in vain and the evening was a disaster.

Xavier could have decided never to have another dinner party. He could have intensified his worrying prior to hosting future entertainments. Instead he looked at how his worrying had not helped him plan the perfect occasion and had made him too strained to enjoy anything. He also realized that he had completely lost his sense of humor. He decided he could learn from what happened. What he learned was that he and his friends' life-styles were too casual to appreciate the structured entertaining he was trying to impose. The next time he invited them to drop over for pizza and all went well.

———80 · Make the Decision

Stop worrying and make a decision. When the decision is made do not keep worrying. Isn't it enough that you worried before the decision? You surely do not have to continue to do so after the decision.

Yolanda went through agonies before she made a decision. She was unable to differentiate between important and unimportant decisions. Each problem carried equal weight for her and each decision was a potential catastrophe that would ruin her life. Even those agonies were not sufficient to keep her from worrying whether or not she had made the right decision. She was never satisfied until she reviewed all the options again, discussed them with many people, and finally lived with the decision long enough to know it was all right.

Zane, on the other hand, looked at his options and made the decision. He never looked back. If the decision didn't work out, he reviewed what options were then available and made another decision he could live with. If all options seemed equally attractive or equally distasteful, he flipped a coin. Don't laugh! Since you cannot foresee the future; since it is impossible to know all the consequences; calling for heads or tails when

51

the coin lands is as good a way to make a decision as any other, and it is a sure way to determine your true desire. If the coin comes up tails and you do not like the choice you called for, you know what decision you really wanted to make. So make it. That is your quick fix for decision making. Toss a coin. If that's too fast for you, go for two out of three. There is nothing inherently better about taking longer to make a decision. In the book "Decision Making" the authors point out that the amount of time spent on a decision is no indicator of its quality.[3] If you must have a decision-making process in order to feel you are doing the right thing, go through the following procedure.

1. Make a list of the pros and cons of the choice.
2. Set a deadline for making the choice.
3. Act as though you have made the decision.
4. Make the decision before or on your deadline.
5. Reward yourself for making the decision.

Now that wasn't so bad, was it?

Yancey could not decide whether to quit his job and accept the offer of another. He decided he could give himself one week to make the decision. He proceeded to look at reasons why he should or should not quit his job. He listed:

CONS	PROS
Old Job	*Old Job*
Bored with the job.	Know job and can do it.
Hate the boss.	Two more years until retirement plan kicks in.
	Close to home.
	Good health insurance.
	Feel secure.
New Job	*New Job*
Ten years before I belong to retirement plan.	Always wanted to do this.
No insurance for six months.	Close to shopping for errands.
Longer drive to work.	I want to do it.

When Yancey looked at the pros and cons he saw that if his priority was security he should stay where he was. When he wrote down that he wanted to make the change he realized his main value in this instance was greater stimulation, new challenges, and the ability to fulfill his potential. He pretended he had made the decision to leave. It felt good. He accepted the job offer and wrote his resignation. To reward himself he bought a new outfit for his first day in his new position.

Did Yancey make the right decision? Who can tell? Maybe the old company went bankrupt. If that happened Yancey would think he made a very smart decision. Maybe the new company went bankrupt. In that case Yancey probably would think he made a stupid decision. In either instance, Yancey would need to realize that he could not know everything, and each decision made always carries an element of chance. Think about it. Next time draw straws to see what you should do.

———81 · Schedule Worry

If you are a worrier you are not going to wake up in the morning, make a resolution to stop worrying, and put it all behind you. You accept worrying as part of you. You may be uncomfortable without it. It is what you do. However, constant worry causes tension. Even when you forget what you are worrying about the anxiety remains. If you feel you must worry you need a technique to worry without experiencing free-floating anxiety. To achieve this, schedule your worrying. A time set aside for you to devote totally to your worries will help you keep them under control. This is easier to do if you write out your worry or worries. This lets you keep track of the things you want to worry about without keeping them on your mind. It will also help you concentrate on your worries when you have a written reminder in front of you.

Set a time and a place to worry. Schedule at least one half hour for this task. Anything less won't do as you will not get in enough worrying time. Do not have your worry time just before you go to bed, and do not have your worry spot in your favorite place. Pick a time that you can keep in your daily schedule on a regular basis. Sit in a comfortable place, but not in your chair. Don't use the chair you habitually occupy for watching television, reading, and visiting.

A designated worry time worked for Zoe. Traditionally she worried all day. After all, there was always something to worry about. She trained herself to hold her worries until 5:00 P.M. She sat on the cellar steps for thirty to forty-five minutes and worried. If she had specific written worries she worked on them. If she didn't she could always find something. This was an excellent technique for her because she could worry, as was her penchant, but the worries did not control her thoughts. She did allow herself a few minutes of worry at other times during the day if she felt she needed the time. However, she was rigid about where she worried. She would not permit herself to worry anywhere but in her private place on the cellar steps. Naturally, she had to adapt this approach to different settings when she was away from home on vacation or business travel.

——82 · Find a Perspective

Are you the only person to ever worry about this? Has anybody else ever coped in similar circumstances? Could your situation be a whole lot worse than it is? Do you see others in more difficult and traumatic situations?

Think about others and their problems. Have they survived? You probably will too.

Think about how bad your problem could actually be. In comparison, does your problem seem less overwhelming? Self-help groups are effective because members realize that there are others with similar problems and they are managing. There is also the opportunity to realize that your problems are not as bad as someone else's problems. In other words, you get a perspective on your worries.

Sara worried herself sick when she got fired. She felt she was the only one to whom this had ever happened. She couldn't tell anyone. She was embarrassed and ashamed. Wandering through the bookstore one day she discovered information on the subject. She read avidly and learned that her experience was not much different from others who had lost their jobs. They had survived, and many had prospered. She started noticing articles about job problems. One successful late night talk show host revealed that she had been fired eighteen times. Sara dared to hope. She began to see her situation as fairly common, not fatal, and that it could be much worse. She put her problem in perspective and became her functional self again.

——83 · Get Away from It

Getting away from the problem is similar to letting it simmer, but is a more aggressive approach to worry. Parents whose grown children live in other parts of the country report relief from worrying about them when they are not part of their day-to-day activity. By the time they hear about what has happened, the problem has been resolved. There is less worrying because the family members do not know what is going on in time to do the worrying. You may not be able to move to a different state to get away from your worries, but you can take vacations, avoid contact with the problem person or place, and focus your time and attention on other things.

Abigail felt she could not go on her planned and paid-for vacation because the organization she presided over was having its annual home show and everything was up in the air. She troubled herself with every detail. She groused when deadlines were not met. She had qualms about all the committee chairpersons. With much persuasion and insistence her family got her to go on her vacation. At first she called one of the home show planners every day to check, remind, and query. As she was told that all was well and as she got more involved in her trip her concerns regarding the organizational event became more remote. When she returned she was mildly disappointed that they had managed so well without her, but learned that they could function without her constant prodding and supervision.

——84 · Learn To Laugh at Yourself

If you cannot see humor in the situation while it is happening, teach yourself to do this by looking at it after it is over. You do realize that if you are reading this you have survived everything you have ever worried about. So lighten up.

Barry worried about his health. One day he felt a little lightheaded while he was driving on the expressway. He decided he was either having a stroke, suffering from low blood sugar, or having a heart attack. He carried his negative thoughts to the logical conclusion of losing control of the car and having a wreck. But this was not enough to worry about. He decided that he would get charged with drunk driving for his erratic behavior. With this in mind he scrawled a note for his rescuers, explaining his perilous physical condition and disclaiming the use of alcohol. At the time he did this he was serious. When he retold his story to someone he trusted he recognized the humor in his runaway worries. A light went on. After that he tried to cut through his wild mental meanderings with a guffaw before they got out of control. When he found he could do that he also found he could enjoy his wonderful imagination and regale people with tales of his fancies.

Barry had a further benefit from his humorous insight. When he started to smile his body relaxed. When he chuckled his mood changed. As he practiced looking for a laugh, he got his mind off his worries.

—————85 · Don't Fight Change

Change is inevitable. You move, age, learn, acquire, replace, remove, correct, and modify.

If you are a person who has difficulty adjusting to every change and would rather fight than switch, you are making life too hard for yourself. Another change is vital for you. That is a change in attitude. See change as opportunity. Change does not mean that problems will go away. It only means that problems may change. But change does bring the promise of new experiences from which you can learn and grow.

You can learn to adjust to change. Those who have had practice in coping with change master the skill of dealing with change. Start by making some changes in your everyday life. Rearrange the furniture. Take a different route to work. Eat and sleep at different times. Do something you have never done before. Embrace change. See it as exciting and challenging, rejuvenating, and enjoyable.

When the post office department changed Candace's zip code and the telephone company changed her area code, she felt as though she was being persecuted. As was her pattern, she pouted and railed against them. She was sure her mail would go astray and her telephone messages would be lost. She knew she would lose friends and business. Her stationery was wrong. How would she let everyone know of the change? Perhaps all this was true. But the change occurred no matter how Candace felt or how much she worried.

Daphne did not like the zip and area code changes any more than did Candace. However, she handled them better. She saw the changes as a reason to contact her friends, update her business files, and get new stationery and business cards in a design she wanted. Instead of worrying she accepted the inevitable change and planned for it with creativity and pleasure.

The problem was the same for Candace and Daphne, but their approach was radically different. Whose do you think was most effective? Which woman had more fun?

———86 · Keep a Prop Around

Is there something that you can look at or do that always elicits amusement? If it works, use it. Keep whatever this is around to distract yourself, change your mood, and get you out of the worrying mode.

Aaron carried a picture of a sanctimonious person's facial reaction after he was caught in a scandal. This always made him snicker.

Amber kept a bottle of magic bubble fluid handy. When she got to worrying she pulled out the wand and made bubbles.

Martha listened to old Spike Jones records. They were so outlandish to her that she forgot to worry while she was enjoying them.

Arthur had a laughing-head. Whenever he shook this battery-operated device and it started to chortle his worries stopped.

Aaron had something to look at. Amber had an activity. Martha and Arthur listened to something. Which of your senses is most likely to respond to a stimulation that takes you away from your worries?

──────87 · Cultivate Optimism

Worrywarts focus on the negatives. Worrying does not prevent problems. Pervasive pessimism causes problems. The pessimist's immune system does not function as well and chronic illnesses are more likely to strike earlier and harder. This is not only because of mood but because the worriers see themselves as unable to effectively change situations through their own actions. They think that anything they do will have negative results. They end up worrying more and not taking the possible positive actions that might help. If this strikes a familiar chord with you use the following to help yourself think more positively.

1. Recognize your beliefs. Everyone has beliefs. Your belief could be that everything always works out for the best. Or it could be that everything will go wrong and that it will go wrong at the worst possible moment.

   The first belief, that all is well, is the optimist's approach. The second is a negative view of life and is embraced by the wary worriers of the world. Which is your belief?

2. Know it is just a belief. You have already accomplished this step because you identified your belief in the first step. A belief is not necessarily based on fact. It is a way

of thinking. Believing something does not make it truth. Synonyms for belief are idea, opinion, faith, feeling, notion, and view. A belief is defined as hope and expectation. You set yourself up for what happens to you with your beliefs. You may as well hope for and expect good things. Optimists get along better than pessimistic worriers. And they are more likeable.

3. Change your negative belief to a positive belief. Record your negative belief and write the opposite, the positive point of view, next to it. Whenever you hear a positive position that refutes your negative notion, write that down too. Read this list regularly until you know the positive side by heart. Whenever the negative belief comes to mind, recall the optimistic information and replace the negative thought with a positive one.

Of course, this takes some work, but it does not take long. You can change your bad (negative) habit in three weeks if you work at it. If you persist in negating your bothersome belief with optimistic facts and ideas, you will notice a change in four days and have a healthy, ingrained habit at the end of three weeks.

Beverly felt she was a pessimistic person. She never got much joy out of life. She thought she was not as good as other people so she could never have the good things in life that they had. A friend was astonished to hear of this belief after she inquired about Beverly's gloomy look. This motivated Beverly to reexamine her belief. She did not know where it came from, only that it was there. She decided she could do something about it since it was a nebulous belief that had no identified source. She started listening to what people said about her and her work. She wrote down the good comments and read them over regularly. Slowly she made inroads into her pessimistic premise about herself. As she focused on good things she became more optimistic. At the end of three weeks she found herself taking good things for granted.

——88 · Developing Serenity

Worry is a habit. If you spend as much time on anything else as you spend worrying you could be an expert in that other thing. For example, if you practiced the piano with the same amount of fervor and time that you give to worrying you would be a top-notch piano player. Apply some of the time you put into worrying into developing serenity.

Path 1 to serenity

Define serenity. What does serenity mean to you? Picture yourself as a serene person.

Path 2 to serenity

Write out all the ways you can think of to chase worries. Put a star near the ones you know will work.

Path 3 to serenity

Say to yourself, as often as needed, "I will think serene, calm, confident thoughts. I will see myself as the serene person I want to be."

These three paths to serenity are to be used simultaneously. One path is not exclusive of the others. Visualize serenity. Know what works for you to effectively dispel your worries. Change your thought pattern from worry to serenity.

Brian was tired of worrying about what people thought of him. Serenity to him meant not going over everything everybody said and did to see if they were approving and accepting of him or critical and rejecting. He pictured himself relaxed around others. He saw himself making decisions without worrying about whether the men and women in his company approved or disapproved. Their opinion was not important. His was.

Brian recognized he had been able to stop, or at least diminish, his worries in the past by recounting good results from contacts with others. He kept reminding himself to focus on that. As time passed and he became more successful in warding off worries he added to his success list. Some of the additions were

—Thinking about compliments he had received.

—Recognizing all that he did well.

—Knowing that going to the theater always cheered him and got his mind off himself.

—He knew his family loved him, so he must be lovable.

At first he kept saying to himself that he would think serene, calm, confident thoughts. Later he did not have to say this phrase as often. Finally he only had to say serene to himself whenever he started to analyze and worry. Brian became the serene person he wanted to be.

——89 · Problem Solving

G. K. Chesterton said, "I do not believe in a fate that falls on men however they act; but I do believe in a fate that falls on them unless they act."

One way to handle problems is to take action. But just taking action without a plan may give you reason to worry more. Here is an action plan.

1. Pinpoint the problem.

Defining the problem is a crucial step. This identifies what you are worrying about and what there is that requires action. A problem is not, "I don't feel good about my neighbor." A problem is, "My neighbor's dogs bark all night and keep me awake."

2. Know your goal.

The goal is what you want to achieve. In this instance it would be that the dogs' barking not keep you awake.

3. Look at solutions.

Brainstorm solutions. Write down anything that comes to mind, including the outrageous. They might lead you to think of other solutions that may be plausible. Some might be:

    a. Get ear plugs.
    b. Soundproof the bedroom.
    c. Call the police.
    d. Kidnap the dogs.
    e. Record the bark and play it back to the neighbor.
    f. Discuss the problem with the other neighbors.
    g. Ask the dogs' owner to address the problem.

4. Analyze the advantages and disadvantages of each approach.

Carefully look at each solution, listing its advantages and disadvantages. Keep your list as the approach you use may not work and you may decide to try another or a combination of approaches.

    a. *Get earplugs.*

ADVANTAGES
1. Won't have to confront the neighbor.
    b. *Soundproof the bedroom.*

DISADVANTAGES
1. They bother my ears.

ADVANTAGES
1. Won't have to confront the neighbor.
2. Good to do anyway because of other neighborhood and household noises.
    c. *Call the police.*

DISADVANTAGES
1. Expense.

ADVANTAGES
1. Someone else can confront the neighbor.

DISADVANTAGES
1. There may not be a law that will help.
2. Don't want neighbor in trouble with the law.

    d. *Kidnap the dogs.*

ADVANTAGES
1. The problem is gone.

DISADVANTAGES
1. Neighbor really loves the dogs.
2. What would I do with the dogs after I got them?
3. It is illegal.
4. Neighbor might get noisier dogs to replace them.

    e. *Record the bark and play it back to the neighbor.*

ADVANTAGES
1. There would be recorded evidence for future use.

DISADVANTAGES
1. Don't really want to harass the neighbor.

    f. *Discuss the problem with other neighbors.*

ADVANTAGES
1. I wouldn't be the only one complaining.

DISADVANTAGES
1. Might stir up trouble and animosity in the

2. The neighbor would see that the dogs are a public nuisance.
3. Others may suggest more solutions.

neighborhood.
2. The other neighbors might think I'm the one in the wrong.

    g. *Ask the dogs' owner to address the problem.*

ADVANTAGES
1. It is the honest, forthright way.
2. The neighbor probably wants to know if there is a problem.

DISADVANTAGES
1. The neighbor may get angry.
2. The neighbor may refuse to do anything.

    5. Decide on the approach.

Keeping the goal in mind, the easiest solution, with the fewest complications is usually the one to pick. Which one would that be? If the one you picked does not work there are several other feasible ways to attack the problem.

    6. Put the approach into action.

As you work on your worries keep the following in mind.

"You can't control the length of your life—but you can control its width and depth. You can't control the contour of your face—but you can control the expression. You can't control the weather—but you can control the atmosphere of your mind. Why worry about things you can't control when you can keep yourself busy controlling the things that depend on you."
—*Author Unknown.*

See also Chapter 3 Stress, Chapter 1 Anxiety, and Chapter 4 Shyness.

• NOTES •

1. Wayne W. Dyer, *Your Erroneous Zones* (New York: Funk and Wagnalls, 1976).
2. Daniel Goleman, "Denial and Hope," *American Health* (December 1984): 54–57.
3. Irving Janis, and Leon Mann. *Decision Making* (New York: Free Press, 1977).

Chapter THREE

STRESS

YOUR BODY TELLS you when you are experiencing stress. Your system has physical, chemical, and mental reactions to situations that frighten, excite, irritate, confuse, or endanger you.

Stress is part of your life. It is not possible for you to lead a stress-free life. Your body is built to respond and you are busy responding to stimulation minute to minute. If you think you perceive an emergency, your juices start flowing whether or not it is a real emergency. In the first six to ten seconds of a sensed emergency your mind and body will react. Your eyes dilate. Muscle tension increases, first in the face, then in the entire body. You hold your breath or overbreathe. Blood stops flowing to the hands and feet and collects in the deep muscles used for running and fighting. You clench your jaw. Your heart rate, blood pressure, skin temperature, sweat glands, gastrointestinal activity, and muscle tension all increase. This is good. Your body is ready for action. You are stimulated, responsive, and on your toes. You are prepared to do a good job.

However, unrelieved stress can be harmful. In these circumstances you may develop hypertension, indigestion, ulcers, backache, heart disease, headache, and emotional upset. If you are in chronic stress your feet and hands are chronically cold.

If stress is infrequent and you can respond and recuperate, no untoward physical and emotional problems result. Feeling constant stress is what makes you sick.

Blanche had responsive emotions. She bragged that she could cry at commercials. Although she was proud of her talent for feeling and expressing herself, she realized that her passionate perceptions were causing her pain. Blanche was not a placid person, and her chemistry was always aswirl as she responded to events in an emotional way. Blanche did not want to change her way to be, but she wanted a better way to manage her manufactured stress. She needed some quick fixes to relieve stress rapidly. Everyone can use a few quick fixes when it comes to handling stress.

Bert worked in a business in which pressure was unrelieved during working hours. Besides having a tense work situation, he could best be described as driven. He was more demanding of himself than any supervisor or situation could be. He always operated on full throttle. Bert's mind whirred with details to check, goals to meet, deadlines to beat, and people to please. A quick fix might help Bert, but he would more likely have to develop a new attitude and life-style to conquer his stress.

Keep in mind that life is 10 percent what you make it and 90 percent how you take it.

• EXERCISES TO RELIEVE STRESS •

Exercise is an excellent means for relieving stress. You have regular stress so planning for regular exercise is planning for your good health. However, for a quick fix you need quick exercises you can do to relieve that unrelieved stress. Make some of the following part of your stress-alleviation repertoire.

———90 • Tense Neck and Shoulders

Place your hands on your shoulders.
Pull your elbows in and back.

This quick fix is effective for those of you who work over a desk or carry heavy objects. Tension seems to lodge in the shoulders. If you do this exercise about ten times at regular intervals you will dislodge some of the accumulated muscle stress.

———91 • Facial Exercise

Wrinkle your forehead tightly and let it smooth out.
Frown, then smile.

Close your eyelids tightly, then let them relax.
Clench your teeth together.
Press your tongue to the roof of your mouth.
Relax.
Let your lips part slightly.

This quickie is good for you if you tend to grind your teeth or get a firm set to your jaw during times of stress. This can be completed in seconds and performed as often as needed.

——92 · Neck and Shoulder Roll

Slowly bend your head forward three times, backward three times, and to each side three times.

Pull your shoulders as far forward as you can, then as far up and as far down as you can.

Repeat three times.

——93 · Arm Roll

Extend your arms and rotate them five times.
Reverse, making larger circles.

——94 · Hand Flexing

Make a fist with each hand.
Stretch your fingers.
Hold to the count of five.

——95 · Stomach Stress Relief

While you are sitting, pull in your stomach.
Breathe normally.
Drop forward.
Lift your toes high, keeping your heels on the floor.
Relax your stomach muscles.
Wiggle your toes.
Circle your feet by rotating them at the ankles.
Tighten your buttocks.
Count to five.

Relax.
Tighten your stomach muscles.
Count to five.
Relax.

Use any or all of these exercises depending on whether stress symptoms settle in your system. If you develop a habit of taking these exercise breaks you will be disrupting your habits that bring on physical stress. Read further and learn about more quick and easy stress releasers.

——96 · Shake It

Shake your right hand.
Shake your left hand.
Let your mouth go slack and shake your head.
Shake your right leg.
Shake your left leg.
Shake your entire body.

——97 · Exercise Your Insides

Say, ha, ha, ha.
Keep it up until you are genuinely laughing.

This will exercise your internal organs, cheer you up, and increase your circulation.

——98 · Relax Your Eyes

Change your focus. Look off into the distance, and blink several times.

Focus close up and blink.

Repeat.

Concentrate on letting your eyebrows and eyelids feel heavy and sag downard with the force of gravity.

Use these exercises regularly if your work is repetitive.

——99 · Stretch

Stand up. Stretch as far as you can in every direction, up, down, left, and right.

I used these exercises as I sat waiting for my delayed flight. They worked. But why was everyone looking at me?

——— 100 · Yawn

Yawning feels good. It is relaxing. Everyone can do it. You do it and you will notice others following suit. Why are yawns catching?

——— 101 · Warm Cold Hands

Rub your hands together briskly.
Let them float warmly to your thighs.
Pick them up and bring them together.
    Blow on your fingers to warm them with the heat from your body.
    Place your warmed hands on a tense or sore spot.
    Feel your warmth relax that part of your body.

——— 102 · Back Relief

With your feet flat on the floor, move to the edge of your chair.
Lean forward until your chest is on your knees.
Let your hands and head dangle.
    Slowly return to an upright position, feeling each of your vertebrae unroll.
    Repeat until the knots are gone.

——— 103 · Beat Something Soft

Pound your pillow. Bat a balloon. Work out any pent-up steam.

——— 104 · Reverse Your Position

Lie on the floor and put the lower part of your legs and your feet on a chair.
    Raise your head.

Place your head back on the floor.
Breathe deeply and relax.

——— 105 · Loosen Up

Swing your arms forward one at a time as though you are swimming.

Now do the backstroke.

Repeat each motion ten times.

Put your hands on your hips and bend at the waist until your upper body is parallel to the floor.

Move from your waist to the left and right.

Repeat ten times.

Raise your arms above your head and bend your knees.

Repeat ten times.

Adapt these simple exercises to your schedule, your needs, and your flexibility. Do not do the bending exercises if you have a bad back. Do not abuse sore body parts.

• PREVENT STRESS •

——— 106 · Start on Time

If you start on time you do not have to play catch up all day long. If you start on time others will notice and will more likely be on time for you. Stop on time too. Control your time instead of letting time control you.

——— 107 · Put Things Off

Not everything has to be done right away. Many things will wait until you get to them. Do not let yourself feel an urgency to do what does not have to be done now. Think about what you can put off. Make a list. Put the list out of sight.

——— 108 · Schedule Fun Times

If you face a task that is decidedly unpleasant (and we all do at times) schedule a reward, a fun time, a time for rest, relaxation, and recreation when it is completed. Then you can look forward to something better, rather than get stuck on the dreaded chore. Following the disagreeable with a pleasant event gives you time to recuperate. This does not mean you have to take a week off every time you have a confrontation with someone. It does mean that you should be nice to yourself on a planned and regular basis. You may not be able to travel to the tropics after every untoward occasion, but you can visit a friend, go swimming, attend a play, go out to dinner, or purchase a small luxury. What are the instant rewards that would please you?

109 · Take Charge

Get up early enough that you are not rushed. Set appointments with people you need to see so they fit into your schedule. Write down what you need to remember so you do not have to keep it all in your mind. Realize that you do not have to keep it all in your mind. Realize that you do not have to be responsible for everything. Get help. Avoid people who annoy you.

110 · What Makes You Uptight?

Identify all the things that make you feel tense, fearful, or disturbed. If you are not sure what they are keep a stress diary for one week noting what upsets you, when it upsets you and how you react. You can exclude some of your stressors from your life. Others you may have to handle in different ways. You may need to change your attitude about many of them. What irritates you? Authority? Loud noises? Speaking in public? Teasing? Criticism? Being ignored? Making mistakes? Not being respected? Wicked people? Angry, weak, or inconsiderate people? Traffic? Waiting? Faulty merchandise? Rowdy children? Disagreements? Note everything that ruffles you. Which can you ignore? Cross those off your list. Those stresses are solved. Ignore them. Star those you can handle through problem solving, setting limits, or getting help or cooperation from others. Take action and settle those aggravations. What you have left are the stresses over which you feel little or no control. Your relief will come from accepting them, looking at them in different ways, or deciding not to get caught up in things you cannot do anything about. You must change your attitude.

How do you change your attitude? Usually not instantly. Attitude changing does not legitimately belong in a book on quick fixes. However, if your attitude does not change, neither will your stress. So it is quicker to go to work on your attitude, no matter how long it takes, than to continue a lifetime of burdensome and bothersome stress over matters that are beyond your control. You may not be able to control the traffic, but you can control your reaction.

1. Recognize that the situation is not your problem and is beyond your control.
2. Accept the fact that you cannot change the people or the events. You can only change yourself.
3. Brainstorm how you might handle the distressing circumstances without causing yourself stress.
   a. Decide it is their problem, not yours.
   b. See the humor in the situation.
   c. Plan not to take the bait.
   d. Figure out a way to perceive it in a more positive light.
   e. Turn whatever is said into something that is to your advantage.
   f. Fix your attention on something else.
   g. You can come up with something better than any of the above. Work at it.
4. Give yourself credit for every time you are not disturbed by the formerly stressful situation.
5. Enjoy your freedom from chronic stress.

——111 · Write It

Carry writing material with you at all times. Have it available where you sit and where you sleep. As thoughts, concerns, and things to do come to mind write them down. When they are out of your mind and on paper you are free of them because you can refer to them as needed. If you keep them in your mind, you constantly check and remind yourself not to forget for fear your ideas and responsibilities might get lost in some corner of your brain.

━━━112 · Take Care of Yourself

Be kind to your body. Eat right. Get enough sleep. Exercise. Have a hobby and other interests. Cultivate supportive friends. Do the things that make you feel good about yourself.

━━━113 · Be Prepared To Wait

Give yourself plenty of time to catch the plane, make the appointment, or run the errand. You may be early, but you will not feel pressured. And if you are early, be prepared to wait. Bring along letters to write, books to read, and anything else you need or want to do. You will enjoy waiting for your appointments because it gives you time to relax and organize and do the things you could not otherwise work into your schedule. See waiting as an opportunity rather than as time wasted. A fact of life is that Americans spend six months of their lives waiting for a red light to change. Accumulated waiting, including time standing in checkout lines and time spent on the telephone "on hold" adds up to five years of your life. So use your waiting for your benefit.

━━━114 · Plan for Stress

Certain times in life are stressful. You can count on these stressful times and plan for them. There is more stress any time there is a change, such as moving or changing jobs. There is more stress during life-style changes such as graduation, marriage, birth of a child, or a death. There is more stress during reversals, such as money problems, car breakdowns, and sickness. Since you know these will happen during the course of your life, be prepared for these events so you can overcome the stress involved, rather than have it overcome you. At the same time you plan ahead, also work at staying flexible because your script will be followed only by you. Others will have their own agendas. The best preparation is to know that change will take place and not always at the planned time in the planned way. Prevent stress by learning to accommodate change. If you haven't had much practice at change, change some thing so you can work at adjusting to it. Review your past life and look for small changes you have successfully incorporated into your lifestyle. Recognize this and use what you learned. If change has been difficult, decide that you are not going to maintain that pattern. Look at how you could have handled the change more serenely. Plan how you will manage similar situations in the future. Never tell yourself that you cannot do it. Always see yourself coping well during stressful times.

Take a look at your family. What milestones are likely to occur over the next few years? What part will you play? How can you be helpful? How can the life event be meaningful for you? What aspects of it will you like? Will there be benefits for you? Change is never all bad. See some of the positive points. Nothing is ever 100 percent good or bad.

Cara always felt she could not face major life changes such as her children leaving home, loved ones dying, or moving to a different home. Consequently, she refused to think about any of those things. She got through each event by pretending it was not happening. Thus she never got any enjoyment when good resulted, was no help to anyone else in the family who was also experiencing stress, and ended up trying to come to terms with her feelings long after everyone else had moved on and made their adjustments. She realized she was always on edge because she was putting all her energy into avoiding stresses that kept coming no matter how much she pretended that life would not change. She decided to face the next event on the family continuum head-on. When her mother became seriously ill and was hospitalized she did not refuse to visit because she could not stand the stress, but went to see her armed with useful approaches. She visited her mother for short periods of time, always delivered cheerful news of the family, and left something that her mother and her caretakers could enjoy. She was so busy planning for her mother's comfort that she forgot about her own stress. She was thrilled to be part of an important family event, rather than a worried nonparticipant. She felt effective. Putting her resolve into practice changed Cara's stress, her family relationships, and her life for the better. The stress of change never paralyzed her again.

——— 115 · Say No

Set boundaries. Your time is yours. Your possessions are yours. Your talents are yours. Time, possessions, and talents are to be shared, but on your terms. If you cannot say no you will have no time, possessions, or talents that you can claim for yourself. If you overcommit yourself, if your possessions are not where you need them when you need them, and if you put all your talents at the disposal of anyone who wants to use them in the way they want to use them, you will be under extreme stress. You will have no control.

Start by setting your priorities. What do you most want to do with your time? Then figure out how much time you have left for what others ask of you. What will you have to cut out? Where do you need to start saying no? Talk about a quick fix! One little word—no.

Who abuses your possessions when they use them? You don't have to let those people use your things anymore. What do you have that you prefer not to share? Keep those things for yourself.

What are you good at? Is giving away what you do well keeping you from putting time into developing a more successful business, marriage, or family? If so, learn to set limits on how much of yourself you can share with people who bring meaning to your life.

Practice saying no. You will find that your life will get better, you will feel better about yourself, others will respect you more, and your stress will decrease sharply.

Douglas wanted people to like him so he tried to do whatever anyone asked of him. What he succeeded in doing was to spread himself too thin, doing lots of things he did not like to do for people and projects he did not care about, and alienating his family. His family wondered why he couldn't give them some of the time he gave so willingly to anyone else who wanted him. Most of the time Douglas did not get good feelings about what he was doing as he was rushed and felt unappreciated and guilty that he neglected his family. On the verge of collapse he stopped doing everything. Although he did this in desperation he found that people did not hate him for saying no. He got a chance to be with and learn about his family, and he felt the love he had so futilely pursued. He liked himself better too.

——116 · Know What Works

Do not fumble along and hope for the best. Note what works for you so you will know what to do when you are under stress. What relaxes and rejuvenates you? How do you cope? What are your successes? Analyze them and learn from them. Be grateful for them. Remember them. Use them.

· QUICK STRESS EASERS ·

——117 · Bake Bread

Homemade bread has to be kneaded. The more you pound and push the better the results. As the bread rises in the pan the stress will lower in your system.

——118 · Cry

Tear ducts are safety valves. Crying can and does ease tension. It is an honest release of feelings.

——119 · Play

A happy stress reliever is play. Play should not be considered frivolous. It can make life enjoyable and save a life that is too stress filled. Play at whatever you like. Remember, it is play, not a competition, not a duty or obligation, but something to do that has only one purpose—fun.

——120 · Brush Your Hair

Brushing your hair reduces the tightness in the muscles of your head. This feels good. The repetitive, soothing motion will lull you into your comfort zone.

———121 · Soak

Fill the tub with warm water, add some bath oil, and soak for fifteen to thirty minutes. Read, listen to slow music, daydream, or simply stare into space.

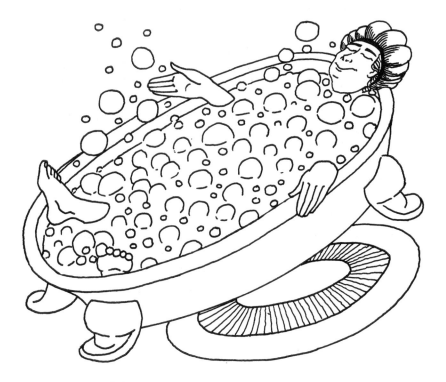

———122 · Do Puzzles

As you solve word or jigsaw puzzles you will get out of your funk and feel satisfaction at your success. Generalize this triumph to your day-to-day living and see yourself solving the puzzles of your life.

———123 · Walk in the Rain

Walking in the rain is refreshing, and invigorating and will give you a new outlook on your stress.

——124 · Fly a Kite

Up, up, and away! Fly a kite and your stress will float skyward with the wind that propels the kite.

——125 · Talk

Don't brood. Call a trusted friend or relative and talk it out. As you put your problems into words you will gain insight and understanding and find relief. Your confidant might have helpful suggestions, but all you really need is a good listener. Verbalizing your problem is enough to help you develop a new perspective.

——126 · Do Something for Others

One of the best ways to take care of your stress, feel good about yourself, and make an important contribution is to do something for someone else. As you volunteer to assist those who need your help, your mind will refocus on areas of interest outside yourself. You will end up feeling terrific because others will admire you for your good works.

——127 · Leave

When a situation feels too stressful walk away from it temporarily. You will function better and more effectively because you took a break.

——128 · Hang a Do Not Disturb Sign

If you need time to decompress, put a do not disturb sign on your door and read, nap, exercise, or do whatever helps you relax. If you do not have a room available, let people around you know when you are off-limits and should not be approached or asked to do another thing. Maybe your signal will be where you sit, or what you wear or a sign to indicate that you have set your boundaries.

——— 129 · Browse

Browse through a department store, flea market, art gallery, museum, or bookstore. Some stores or museums may interest you more than others. Visit those for pleasure and as a way to get away from pressure.

——— 130 · Sort Out, Throw Away

Clean out a drawer, a closet, or a file cabinet. As you rid yourself of clothes, items, and papers you no longer need you are clearing out the clutter in your life. As you get rid of what you do not want or use, see it as symbolically letting go of your stress.

——— 131 · Listen to Someone Else

Pay attention to what someone else is saying. Concentrate on the words being used and the message. Don't think about what you want to say next. Keep your mind on the speaker. Notice how much less stressful it is to do only one thing at a time. Generalize this to other situations and work at doing one thing at a time.

——— 132 · Go to School

Take a course, not just any course. Take one on a subject you have always wanted to know more about. It might be a class on sailing, jewelry making, or astronomy. The best would be for you to find an interest that becomes a relaxing pursuit.

——— 133 · Dress Comfortably

Wear clothes that feel good. Wear clothes that you think make you look good. Toss out clothes that are too tight or feel wrong.

——— 134 · Take a Nap

Forget all of it. Curl up and sleep. There is no rule that you may only sleep at night. Sleep at various times and in various places. Are you tired of driving? Pull over and snooze. Are you worn out with work? Take a break by putting your head on your desk and taking a few winks. Of course, sleep in safe places—and don't let the boss see you.

——— 135 · Rearrange and/or Redecorate

Fix up your office or your home or one part of the place where you live to give yourself a feeling of living well. Gather your favorite possessions. Use the colors you like. Make it a place that helps you feel good and relaxes you.

——— 136 · Cut Out the Noise

Noise is stressful. Cut down on unnecessary and excessive noise in your surroundings. If you work or live with noise, take quiet breaks and feel your stress unravel.

——— 137 · Visit Your Favorite Place

Whenever you feel stress creeping up on you, mentally leave for your favorite place. Imagine the scene in your mind. See all that you like about it. Hear the reassuring sounds of the birds, waves, or wind. Inhale the soothing smells of trees, water, or home cooking. You can go wherever you want in your mind. Have one or several special places.

——— 138 · Step Back

Get away from your work, your stress, your worry. Gaze out the window. Walk around the house or the office. Stroll down the hallway or sidewalk.

——— 139 · Change Gears

Pick up a short-term project, something you can finish in ten to thirty minutes. Stop that which is stressful, change gears, and have the satisfaction of a completed task.

——140 · Pamper a Plant

A plant in your work place is a nice touch. Use it as a stress alleviator. Dust it. Shine it. Water it. Pick off the dead leaves. Stir the soil. Talk to it.

——141 · Peel an Orange

This is a break that takes a little more than just popping a morsel into your mouth. Peel the orange. Feel the texture. Whiff the aroma. Enjoy the tang.

——142 · Yell

Roll up the windows of your car and yell as loudly as you can. Say everything you've always wanted to say about everybody and everything using whatever language best expresses your thoughts. If you aren't in your automobile, go to the basement, lock yourself in the bathroom, or head for the woods. When it is all out, smile.

——143 · Water Your Wrists

Run cold water on your wrists for a quick refresher. Use warm water to increase the temperature in your extremities and soothe your system.

——144 · Recall Compliments

Remember all the compliments you have received and appreciate them. Go one step further and accept all those remarkable points as the true you.

——145 · Play with Your Pet

Pet your pet. Teach it a trick. Take it for a walk. Tell it all your troubles.

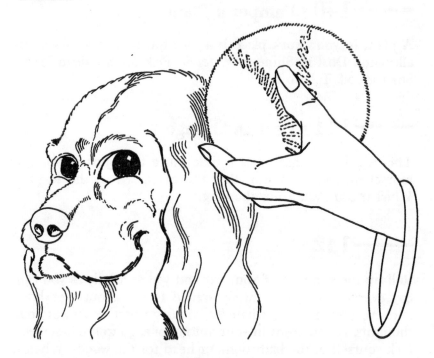

——146 · Sort Out Your Commitments

Know what you have to do and what you chose to do. If you do not have to do something you really do not want to do, reevaluate if you really should do it. Make two lists. What are you doing because you feel an obligation? What are you doing because it is actually required and necessary? If you are doing it because you want to, realize it is your choice. Change your attitude accordingly.

——147 · Use the Environment

Take a drive on a seldom traveled road. Chop trees. Saw wood. Go fishing, boating, camping, or biking. Sit by a stream.

• SEASONAL STRESS •

Holidays are supposed to be a time of good cheer. That expectation is the part that makes them the most stressful. When you are told that you should be experiencing the most wonderful events of the year and you are tired, frustrated, and unhappy, the message and the mind-set are far apart. Major disappointment and stress result.

There are common themes of stress and distress during these special times. You are not alone in these problems. But there are ways to get through the holidays, not only intact, but with a modicum of pleasure. Let's look at some methods for managing seasonal stress.

HOLIDAY PLANNING, PREPARATION, AND PARTIES

One of the problems with holiday planning is getting caught up in all the hoopla. You end up wanting to do it all and have it all. This means taking on more to do than there is time in which to do it, taking in more events than there is energy to include, and wanting everything perfect for all involved. This is an impossible task. It never works out as the pictures in the magazines portray it. To keep holiday stress at a minimum you must start with your planning.

━━━148 • Get Away

Darcy survived holidays by planning to be away when the major ones occurred. Cruises over Christmas and New Year's were her forte. She left the planning and preparations to the staff on the ship while she enjoyed whatever they offered.

━━━149 • Control by Planning

Chester and his family met together to plan their holidays. Each person selected one thing he or she most wanted to do. That is what the person did. If something extra came up the family would reevaluate to see if it should be included, substituted for another event, or put on the list for next year.

——— 150 · Develop Your Own Traditions

Ella was always morose during holidays as she had no relatives with whom to share them. She overcame her depression when she overcame her notion that holidays had to mean family and family traditions. She included people in her planning who were also alone and developed her own traditions that fit her style.

——— 151 · Do It Ahead

Since Ernest wanted to do it all he carried on his holiday preparation all year round. He got cards ready, his gifts purchased, his cooking completed, and his decorations planned so that by the time each special day arrived he could relax and participate in as many events as his time and energy allowed.

——— 152 · Assign Jobs

Faye refused to do it all herself. Everybody had a responsibility at every family gathering. Once established, each person's participation became a part of the enjoyment and tradition.

——— 153 · Pare It Down

Frank figured out how to enjoy himself without being overwhelmed by deciding what was important to him. He stopped sending Christmas cards (few people noticed), declined all cocktail parties (he was uncomfortable with strangers and small talk) and did not worry about cleaning his house to a spotless state. He did less preparation and had less stress.

——— 154 · Please Yourself

When Fred discovered he could not please everyone, he also realized he was not happy with the way his holidays were going. He decided that he should concentrate on pleasing himself. He found that others were no less happy with him than they had been previously. He was a lot more happy with himself after he set his own priorities.

———155 · Do for Others

Leola felt an emptiness during the holidays. She expected more and was always disappointed. She remedied the hollowness she felt by putting her holiday planning and preparation into doing for those who could not do for themselves. She visited nursing homes, donated toys for underprivileged children, served food at the Salvation Army, and helped decorate the hospital's emergency room. She enjoyed the recognition and gratitude she received. She also felt that she got more out of the giving than the recipients did from the receiving. Leola's holiday stress was turned into true holiday spirit.

———156 · Do It When It Is Convenient

Dwight liked everything the holidays brought to his life, but he did not like having to enjoy them during such a compressed period of time. He fixed this time crunch by giving his parties at less busy times of the year, visiting family when the transportation system was not overloaded, and sending cards and notes throughout the year.

———157 · Attitude Adaptation

When you are feeling overcommitted, back off or back out. Failing that, look at it as something you want to do rather than as something you have to do. You have the extra energy to do what you want to do.

A positive attitude will make all the difference in the world. It will make the event more fun and less stressful. While you are at the function concentrate on the here and now. Worrying about what you still have to do or have to do next will not make the party go faster and it will give you less enjoyment and more stress.

What about those people with whom you have to socialize   **85** and would rather not see and those who always caused problems? Try some of the following approaches:

——158 · Sane Socializing

Remind yourself that the encounter is time limited.

Avoid the people you do not like and hang out with those you do.

Do not bring up controversial topics that are guaranteed to get a rise out of certain people. Avoid confrontations.

Be socially polite but get away from the people who make you uncomfortable.

Say no to invitations to places and with people that are toxic to you. Do not invite those people to your house either.

Leave early after making a creditable excuse.

See if you can find out something interesting about someone you always steered away from. Consider it a treasure hunt.

Stand firm and try to figure out what these people do that you find boring, disgusting, or enraging. Think of it as an exercise in self-discovery.

Oma always wanted the special family occasion the media played up. Instead, she got the holiday from hell. Her father invariably got drunk. Her mother cried. Her aunt flirted with Oma's husband. Her grandmother accused her of neglecting her parents. Her husband would storm out of the house after her uncle told him he was a dummy for the way he handled his money. Her sisters never helped with the dishes. Her brothers ignored the whole thing and went outside and played horseshoes with the brothers-in-law. Everybody left angry, upset, and full of stress except maybe the brothers and the brothers-in-law. It took therapy for Oma to realize that the only thing she could change about her family was the way she handled it. This she did. Oma and her family went to her parents' home for a couple of hours before dinner and left. Thus they were able to miss the drinking, arguing, complaining, and crying. They had a pleasant, relatively stress-free encounter that did not mar the holiday.

Van was uncomfortable at office parties and always looked

for excuses to get out of them. He survived them by being friendly, and polite, and leaving at the first opportunity.

Tyrone always enjoyed Martha's company. He invited her to go with him to parties he would not otherwise welcome. Since he knew he would have a good time with her, this changed his attitude and stress level.

Gail knew she was a patsy for a certain acquaintance. This woman could manipulate her into doing anything. She dreaded running into her and wondered why she was so vulnerable to her. She took advantage of a social setting to figure it out and found it time well spent. She learned to say no without making the excuses the woman never acknowledged. She recognized how guilt and fear motivated her. To avoid a confrontation she invariably got swept up in the other person's plans. A much happier and more insightful Gail emerged from that party. This helped lower her stress level. This is not a common way to spend time at a party, but it was the right way for Gail.

HOLIDAY SHOPPING

Some of you love to shop for presents for people. Some of you hate it. No matter how you feel about it, shopping often takes more time and money than you really want to put into it. Gift-giving quick fixes follow:

——**159** · **Shop at sales throughout the year.**

——**160** · **Agree on how much you will spend per gift.**

——**161** · **Give magazine subscriptions or have gifts sent from catalogs so you do not have to wrap and mail or deliver.**

——**162** · **Draw names.**

——— 163 · Discontinue gift giving and contribute to a charity instead.

——— 164 · Agree that everybody has what they want and need and plan no gift giving.

Jessica and Michael worked in the same company. The company laid off both of them. They explained to everyone with whom they generally exchanged gifts that they would not be doing so that year because of their difficult economic conditions. People readily understood. Interestingly, the gift giving was not reinstated after Jessica and Michael went back to work and were more economically secure. Everybody appreciated the end of that tradition.

Matthew's family drew names. Everybody got a gift. It added to the festivities as each person tried to guess who drew their names.

John and Megan fought bitterly every Christmas as John spent more on gifts for his family than Megan was able to spend on hers. Their anger was real and persistent. It ruined the holiday season for them. It came up again and again throughout the year whenever they argued about anything. They finally solved the dilemma by having John buy gifts for both sides of the family, getting identical presents for each family counterpart.

Elizabeth loved to shop and spend money. She indulged this extravagance all year round by attending sales. Whenever a present was needed for anybody she chose from her stock of gifts on hand. No shopping or money stress for her.

James did not shop. He gave everybody money. Most people were glad to get it. One year he ordered fruit for his friends and relatives. The company sent the orders directly to the recipients' homes.

Do what you have to do to get out of the nightmare of shopping. Be honest about your financial status. If you do not want to tell others, at least be honest with yourself. Do not make purchases to impress others. You will be happier throughout the year if you consider your own circumstances and act accordingly. If others want to spend more and give more, respect that as their choice, not as an action that obligates you to do the same.

If you have no money to buy gifts and you want to do something that shows thoughtfulness, prepare a jar of self-esteem. On separate small sheets of paper write out the qualities you admire in the person. Put these in the jar.

Offer to take a person somewhere, baby-sit for the person, clean his or her house, or do for them what they hate to do for themselves. Host a dinner party in his or her honor.

Gift giving may be an ordeal, but being on the receiving end may also be difficult. Gifts for birthdays, anniversaries, weddings, and seasonal events are often opened in public. What do you do? You look pleased and say, "Thank you for your thoughtfulness." If the present can be exchanged, feel free to do that. Otherwise tell yourself that it did not cost you anything so what difference does it make. Do not make a problem for yourself or the giver. Be gracious and let it go. Fretting brings on stress.

If you take care of yourself throughout the holidays, stresses will not accumulate and you will avoid the postholiday blues.

See also, Chapter 1 Anxiety, Chapter 2 Worry, and Chapter 4 Shyness.

Chapter
FOUR

SHYNESS

IF YOU IDENTIFY yourself as a shy person, you probably feel that other people seem to have more fun than you do. And you are probably right. You may think that other people do not give you the recognition you deserve. You may be correct. To change these feelings and facts, new behaviors are needed. These more effective behaviors can be identified. It is possible to substitute new behaviors for old ones. There are quick fixes that will bring immediate rewards. However, the quick fixes have to become habit to bring permanent rewards.

• SYMPTOMS •

Everyone feels shy from time to time. There is no one who has not been intimidated in certain circumstances or with certain people. Facing new situations, meeting awe-inspiring figures or speaking in public can bring out shy, self-conscious feelings in everyone. This is normal shyness that is a part of the human condition. At these times it is common to experience the symptoms of anxiety, fear, and stress such as racing pulse, pounding heart, butterflies in the stomach, trembling, blushing, perspiring, and problems swallowing. When shyness becomes more than an infrequent unpleasant feeling it becomes a major motivator in your life.

Shy people often have difficulty thinking clearly and communicating effectively in the presence of others. This means that their contributions, opinions, and ideas are underrepresented in any work or social situation in which people are brought together and expected to function as a group. Shy people may go along with the prevailing notion even though they do not like it, it is against their better judgment, and it may be dangerous or contrary to their own interests. They may be so self-occupied in a group situation that they cannot keep up with the discussion or sort out the important facts. They will defer to those in greater authority and consequently suffer from poor morale and lack of self-confidence because of their inability to speak up. They see others as doing better than they are doing. They compare themselves to others and see themselves coming off poorly in the comparison. They shy away from confrontations, competitions, or involvements that would require self-revelation.

Shyness is one cause of stress. It may be an important contributor to stress for some people. Researchers at Stanford University found that 42 percent of two thousand people interviewed labeled themselves as shy.

If you are one of the 42 percent, you may want to take action to overcome your shyness because shy people do not make as much money, do not get the jobs they want, and do not get promoted as often as nonshy people. They tend to be lonely because they do not have the friends they want either.

Shy people blame themselves for the behavior of others. If a store clerk is rude to them they think that they did something wrong rather than think the clerk was having a bad day. On the other hand, shy people do not take credit for success. If someone thanks them for an entertaining evening, they cannot believe that they had anything to do with making it go well. They assume it was luck or someone else's influence that made everything come together.

The shy among us use body language that keeps people away. They avoid eye contact, speak softly, smile less, and look downward. They keep a greater physical distance between themselves and other people. Since they defer to others to initiate conversations, they often end up with no one to talk with and feel more intensely self-conscious and shy. They worry about what other people think of them. Since shy people have such intense self-consciousness, they think that others notice them and evaluate them as they do themselves.

A small number of people are born with a tendency toward shyness. Others get stuck in shyness because of what happens to them during their lives. Others are shy at some times during their lives, but not at others. Shyness peaks in the teenage years.

Our culture conspires to make people shy. Children are taught to be quiet, polite, and well-behaved. Overly vivacious and outspoken people are not appreciated. Modesty is seen as a virtue. People who are different are criticized and not readily accepted. Retiring, private people are often called shy when they may be acting out of preference instead of shyness. Training and labeling can create shy, self-reproaching people.

Others may misinterpret the behavior of shy people. They may see them as antisocial, stuck-up, or rude, or unfriendly because they are withdrawn, unsure of themselves, and unable to reach out to others. On the plus side, they are also perceived as good listeners, modest, reserved, and easy to be around. There is a mystique about shy people. They are loyal friends. They are thoughtful. The shy person can keep the good aspects of the trait while doing away with the unwanted characteristics of shyness.

Shyness does not have to last. It is not a permanent condition. It can be cured and you can cure it. Just as you learned to play the guitar and the game of golf or other skills, you can become socially adept, overcome self-consciousness, and conquer shyness. By using quick-fix techniques shy people can become more confident and see a change in their behavior in a week. Ongoing work is required to make the changes lasting.

——— 165 · Structure Situations

You will feel more comfortable in structured situations in which your role is clearly defined than in unstructured situations in which you have to find something to do with yourself. For your first venture, plan your activity carefully so you will feel secure. Be a greeter at a party, agree to pass the drinks, be in charge of the guestbook at an open house, or pass out the publicity brochures at a health fair. Do something that you are comfortable doing and that also gives you maximum contact with people. Help nursing home residents get to and from activities.

Teach someone how to read. Be a cashier at the hospital gift shop. Notice your ability in your role and how people respond positively to you. Having a responsibility and a plan will help you feel comfortable with being responsive as you will have the structure to make it easy.

Nicole did not have to go out of her way to make contacts because, as a waitress, she was involved with people all of the time. She, however, saw this as work and not a social situation. She figured she was accepted and effective in the restaurant setting because she did her job responsively and efficiently. It had nothing to do with her shyness and the difficulty she had handling herself socially. When Nicole could give herself credit for being able to talk with strangers, move among a group of people she had never seen before, recognize and remember regular customers, and see her ability to think on her feet, she took her first step in overcoming her shyness. She started giving herself positive messages and she started recognizing that she was functional around people. Whenever she became tense in a social situation, she reminded herself of her skill with the restaurant customers. That thought gave her more confidence in social settings. If she felt more intense pressure, she gave herself her role in the workplace and saw people as restaurant patrons. This gave the occasion the structure she needed to feel comfortable.

——166 · Just for Today

Set your goals for one day.
- —Just for today you can greet everyone you meet.
- —Just for today you will smile all the time.
- —Just for today you will be impulsive.
- —Just for today you will think positive thoughts.
- —Just for today you will not care what anybody else thinks.
- —Just for today you will express your opinion whether or not anyone else agrees with you.
- —Just for today you will be courageous and unafraid.

Do not try to do these all at once or every day. Pick one and do it just for one day. Note your successes. Note the responses from others. Enjoy the sensation of doing the one thing you pick just for the day.

Joshua decided that he wanted a break from shyness even if it was only temporary. He vowed to make a contribution to every conversation he was part of or could get into. He did this at work, at the gym, at the laundromat, and when he was standing in line at the bank. He knew he only had to do it for the one day. He found that people were generally responsive and pleasant and discovered that he enjoyed himself. Whenever he felt stifled by his shyness, he performed another Just For Today exercise. The more he did this the better he felt about himself. Soon his shyness no longer ruled him.

──── 167 · Meet Somebody New

Even though meeting a new person is an event that makes many people feel shy, particularly if that person is of the opposite sex, there are some who enjoy it and go out of their way to do it. You need to practice being one of those who can meet and greet with aplomb to make an inroad into your shyness. Find someone you have never met at work, in your neighborhood, at the stores you frequent, or anywhere, and introduce yourself. Do this once a week. You will soon catch on to the fact that people are flattered to be singled out and you will be able to have a positive thought each time you recall doing this. Do not concentrate on your nervousness. Concentrate on the fact that you approached another person and the person was pleased.

Lindsey was a regular customer at the library. The librarian who usually helped her often made comments that evidenced interest in the books she checked out. Lindsey picked her for an introduction. She said that she was glad for her running commentary on the books and would like to introduce herself to her because they had been meeting like this for so long. The librarian was obviously gratified. After that their interaction became more personal. A warm, pleasant relationship continued.

──── 168 · Notice Similarities

It is hard for a shy person to think of anything to say. What comes to mind is rejected because it seems inane or too simple. Consequently, many of the quick fixes in this book are specifically about what to say to people in order to get over the first conversational hurdle. They may be inane or simple, but they are examples of appropriate small talk that regularly takes place in social situations.

People are happy to be singled out. People enjoy hearing that what they choose is also favored by others. Examples of this abound:

Wenonah was at a conference. At the break she saw another participant select the black cherry soda. She commented that she liked that flavor too. The woman responded that she hadn't tried it before and asked if it was good. A conversation ensued.

Gary sat next to a man in the airplane who was reading a magazine Gary subscribed to. He remarked that he read the magazine regularly and added what he really liked about it. His seatmate answered that he read it monthly and shared Gary's interest.

The same type of conversation can take place in the grocery store, at work, at the flower shop, or at the meeting of a club.

——169 · Add One More Thing

You will notice from the last quick fix that neither the shy person nor the person addressed let the conversational ball drop. There is nothing automatic about this, nor is it a secret that only a few people know. The principle is easy to understand. You add one more fact, opinion, or feeling. In each of these examples another piece of information was added. Wenonah's conversation partner asked if the drink was good. Gary's seatmate shared that he read the magazine regularly. It was then up to Wenonah and Gary to enlarge further on the topic. Wenonah could say what she liked about the drink or when she discovered it, or bring up a new subject by recommending another taste treat. Gary could ask his seatmate if he had a subscription to the magazine, or if he read a certain column, or talk about an article they could discuss further.

This is how socializing takes place. Innocuous, probably uninteresting topics are thrown out and talked about until something more intriguing results. The trick is to hang in there with the small talk until you arrive at the more stimulating part of the conversation.

When she was asked where she was from, Lila answered Pennsylvania and included the facts that her parents lived there and were dedicated football fans. The respondent then had the choice of pursuing several topics including Pennsylvania, parents, and football. It could also be hometowns, families, or another sport. In this way you get to a shared theme of mutual interest. By that time your fascination with the exchange can be such that you are beyond your shyness and involved in the discussion.

170 · Ice Breakers

Be prepared with small talk. Know that it is always safe to bring up the topics of weather, children, where people grew up, and hobbies. These topics are used as ice breakers. They lead to a more serious conversational engagement or to the decision to move on and talk with someone else. Ice breakers do not have to be the routine subjects used since the beginning of time, but they have stood the test of time. The cave dwellers probably put a lot of conversational energy into talking about the weather, children, where they lived, and what they did.

You do not have to start with these topics if you have other ideas. Read the newspapers and ask or offer comments on the news of the day. Prepare interesting anecdotes and tell them. Make sure the comments and anecdotes are short and to the point so you do not get nervous and the interest of the listeners does not lag.

Headlines that start conversations are political scandals, traumatic accidents, sports competitions, and human interest stories. Asking for opinions or if someone has read the article gets the conversation started. Further explanations and questions keep it going.

Stories about pets, children, work, or anything humorous or a joke on yourself are good.

Tell about the time the cat jumped in the car and went home with your in-laws.

Children frequently make comments that must be repeated, **97** such as when little Hugh said that everyone would know his aunt wasn't his mother because his mother would never wear a hat like the one his aunt had on.

The time your coworker at the rehabilitation center thought the job applicant was a patient and sent her back to be examined by the doctor can be made into an uproarious story.

And don't hesitate to tell about the time you got locked out of the house in your shocking pink baby doll pajamas, tried crawling in through the window, and were approached by a policeman.

Others will enjoy your stories. They will trigger memories and you will get to listen to them tell of their amusing episodes.

——— 171 · Self-Talk

Shy people think negative thoughts. They think they will fail when they speak. They think they will be rejected. They think they will have a miserable time. So they do. They program themselves. It is just as easy and much more fun to supplant those negative thoughts with positive thoughts. This means changing the negative self-talk to positive self-talk. Changing is the operative word. The only way to change is to practice the positive statements instead of staying in the unproductive negative rut.

We all talk to ourselves. Monitor what you are saying to yourself. Be nice to yourself. Say nice things. If you can fill your mind with negative junk, you should be able to manage some positive suggestions. It is important to make your positive self-talk consistent so you learn new messages that lead to high self-regard.

Start by noticing what you say to yourself. Then write out the opposite or positive statement that contradicts the negative thought.

I can't speak in a group.	I always have something interesting to say.
I hate parties.	I'll have a good time. Something interesting will happen.
I never know what to say.	I have lots of things to say.
I get paralyzed with fear.	There isn't anything to be afraid of. I am relaxed.

Also learn to do situational self-talk. When you need to complain about the meal served in a restaurant, the way the bank handled your account, or the mechanic's treatment of your car, tell yourself that you have the right to complain and can be assertive and effective.

Ivy agreed to meet her boyfriend Robert's parents. She knew she would be a dud and they would think she was a loser. She countered her negative thoughts with statements such as that Robert loved her and his parents would too, and that she was comfortable with Robert and could also be relaxed with his parents.

——172 · Make Telephone Calls

Once a day make a business call, get all the information you want, then keep the person on the line and ask one more ques-

tion. Check with the telephone information operator, then ask for address verification. Call the reference librarian, ask if the library has a certain book, and request the name of the author. Telephone the bank to determine its interest rates and ask what other investment programs the bank has.

Hope sincerely wanted to know the price of a new car. She also sincerely wanted to prove to herself that she could keep a stranger on the line for a full five minutes. She asked for other specifics about the car, the warranty, what was included as standard equipment, financing, what tests and studies had been done on performance and safety, and what kind of help she could expect from their service department. She had a successful twenty-minute interview and felt very good about her ability. She continued to do this with other business concerns until the exercise was no longer a challenge for her.

——— 173 · Get Your Feelings To Match the Facts

A problem for you may be the label people stuck on you. Incredibly, you believe them and continue to apply it to yourself. If you were once shy you are likely to always think of yourself as shy even though no one else would notice this trait in you. Shyness may no longer be part of your responses or behavior, but you may continue to identify yourself as a shy person. It is time to change your self-image and see yourself as a confident, socially able person who no longer reacts in shy ways. Get your feelings to match the facts. When you feel shy remind yourself that others do not see you as shy, and that their perceptions are true.

Jason was shocked when Michelle explained that she was shy. Jason saw her as outgoing, poised, and assertive. If he were to give her a one-word description he would have called her raucous. She was comfortable talking in a group, expressing her objections, and was good at telling jokes and making people laugh. She did not appear shy. Jason questioned Michelle to learn that she had been a shy child who had overcompensated, but had settled into being a well-socialized, life-of-the-party type. Michelle needed to discover that the shy label no longer applied to her. If she had to define her major behavior around others she could say she was friendly. Jason suggested this fact to her. She beamed with understanding and set about letting her feelings about herself reflect the real Michelle.

Ryan was painfully shy in his youth but had long since put

that stage behind him. He did not think or act shy, but now and then old shy habits restrained him from doing what should be easy or enjoyable. When he became aware that this was happening to him he understood why he resisted making telephone calls, put off lodging legitimate complaints and had to be dragged to cocktail parties. Old habits die hard. Whenever he felt himself digging in his heels for no apparent reason he reminded himself that he no longer had to act out of shyness. Life became easier and more spontaneous for him.

———174 · Take a Survey

When shyness dominates your behavior and stops you from enjoying a social occasion, bypass the shy feelings by using a technique to keep yourself from being tongue-tied. Go to the dinner, holiday, office, or cocktail party armed with a survey question. Ask the people around the table or go from group to group to obtain opinions about a topic that is of general interest. People will respond with curiosity and animation. It will give them something to discuss too. They will look forward to the results of your informal, unscientific survey. You will get positive attention. Your survey question can be humorous, serious, or timely. It can be:

1. What is your favorite color? Is it true that men prefer blue?
2. How many times do you go to the grocery store each month?
3. If you could have anyone you wanted for (boss, president, mayor, friend, neighbor, spouse, child), who would you pick?
4. What do you most hate to do?
5. What is your biggest time waster?
6. If you could only have one more meal, what would it be?
7. What is your pet peeve?
8. What do you prefer for a pet?
9. What is the best place for a vacation?

What would you like to ask? You can think of more timely, humorous, and intriguing questions.

———175 · Watch Your Body Language

When you look eager and interested, people will approach you. If you look away, distinterested or withdrawn, people will stay away. They will take their cue from you. They will not want to risk rejection if you look as though you do not want company.

Start with two crucial nonverbal signals. Smile. Make eye contact. Keep smiling. Keep eye contact. There are other physical actions that will help you appear less shy, but smiling and looking directly at the person will take you a long way. If you can't manage to look others in their eyes fix your gaze on their noses. But don't stop smiling; look interested and receptive.

Nod your head to show you are listening. Speak loudly enough to be heard. Direct your comments to a specific person. Reach out. Touch people. Lean forward. Move closer. Shy people tend to keep more distance, speak softly, and look at the floor. Do not do these things. Practice your open, fascinated (and fascinating) look in the mirror until you achieve one that looks good to you. Then practice it until it comes naturally. If you have trouble with eye contact, practice with a friend or family member, or even your dog, until you can do it without flinching. Just don't get so good at it that people feel you are staring at them and they get uncomfortable.

Heather was ready to give up. She was not going to go to any more dances or parties as no one ever asked her to be their partner or came over to sit with her. She figured she wasn't fit for the social scene. She decided to drop out. Please note the frame of reference here. Heather blamed herself. She saw herself as not fit for the social scene, not that the social scene did not suit her. There is a big difference here. Anyone can decide he or she does not like to attend events that involve a lot of people and require person-to-person contact. That is not shyness, that is a preference. Heather, however, wanted contact with people, but she felt she was not able to function properly in their company. She could not manage to make social gatherings work for her.

One evening, at a dance, Heather found herself interested in a young man. His manner and clothing style drew her attention. She couldn't stop looking at him. To her amazement, he seemed drawn to her too. He asked her to dance. Heather was ready to write this off to fate until a friend called her unusual behavior to her attention. The friend told Heather that she had never seen her give so much concentration to another person and be so energized. Heather then thought that it might have been her dancing partner who brought out this side of her. However, she had to acknowledge that she was different before she danced with him. In this way Heather learned that her nonverbal actions changed how others saw her and led to her feeling socially able. She worked at this. It did not require talking. It only required that she look happy to be there and glad to see the people. She left her wallflower self-image behind.

——176 · Rehearse

Stop the mental picture of yourself as a cringing, perspiring, blushing person who hangs back. See yourself doing exactly as you would like to do. See yourself accepting compliments, speaking spontaneously, meeting people, and making presentations. If you find you are failing to meet your new expectations, mentally review how you will do it the next time. Do not keep going over what you did wrong. Get rid of that mental image. Picture success. Rehearse your ideal in your mind. Always imagine yourself succeeding.

——177 · Write a Script

To help yourself over the first few minutes of a telephone call or social encounter write out what you plan to say. Depending on the situation, you can read from your script or memorize your part. This will get you started. You can keep the conversation going by responding to what the other person says. You can quit when you get what you want or the topic has been talked out. Don't worry about being original or profound. Use familiar clichés. Everybody understands and is comfortable with them. They are predictable. They are pat responses. It is not too challenging. They will do fine until something better comes along. Ask, "How are you?" Answer, "I'm fine." Say, "Nice day isn't it?" Respond, "Yes, it feels great." These are definitely used phrases, but they continue to be part of ongoing social interactions.

———178 · Write Your Thoughts and Ideas

You can compensate for your inability to verbally express yourself by writing your thoughts and ideas. People will consider it charming and be pleased with this extra effort. Send cards. Write letters. Leave notes. You can communicate well through the written word as it is more precise than that which is spoken.

You can use writing at work too. Write memos to express and explain your ideas. You will get more credit for a comprehensive thoughtful proposal that is written than for verbal suggestions. This also gives your supervisor or coworkers a better opportunity to consider your ideas. Although you may be writing instead of speaking because you are shy, the bottom line is that it is frequently a better approach.

———179 · Give Compliments

What you say is important. Shy people tend to neglect putting their thoughts into words as they feel no one will be interested in what they have to say or it isn't worth mentioning. To find out how important your ideas are, start giving compliments. Promise yourself that you will give three compliments a day. You will notice that people pay attention to nice things that are said about them. Their countenance will brighten and they will hear every word you say. People like hearing good things about themselves and they will think good things about you for being so observant. Compliments can be on anything from appearance to possessions to family members to projects to performances. Go out of your way to compliment a boss or a speaker or someone who gets few compliments because he or she has a position that seems to be above that need. That person will appreciate it and you will feel more powerful for having done it.

Decide to accept compliments too. When someone compliments you on anything from your hairdo to your car, say thank you and express your pleasure that the person noticed. Just a thank you is sufficient, but if you want to keep the conversation going, explain that your hair is that way because it is easy to care for or your car has gotten you back and forth to work for many years. The person then has the opportunity to say more if he or she wants to continue the exchange or can leave if all the person wanted to do was express admiration or appreciation.

Face it, modesty is not necessarily a virtue.

——180 · Go Places

You will not get over your shyness by sitting home alone. Thinking positive thoughts, having a script, rehearsing, and smiling are all excellent activities, but they need to be put into practice in the real world. The world will not come to you. You must reach out and have experiences. Vow that you will go out three times a week. Going out does not mean that you go to the drive-in teller at the bank. Going out means that you have a social interchange of some kind or are with a group of people.

In a flood of determination Kim signed up for an adult education class, bought a ticket to the concert series, and joined the camera club. All these controlled activities gave her opportunities to practice her social skills.

Kim asked at least one question or made one comment in each class she attended, always greeted her classmates, approached them at the break, and said good-bye at class closing. It took no time for her to feel comfortable and spontaneous as they were all strangers and all wanted to be accepted.

At the concert series she found herself with like-minded individuals and saw the same people at each performance. The first time she went prepared with comments, but soon found it easy to speak to her new acquaintances about the music.

The camera club was ready-made for a shy person because each member had an established interest that was the same as the others. They compared, asked questions, and developed skills. Since Kim was personally involved in this hobby she was animated as she eagerly learned more. This gave Kim confidence to be in a group because she felt included. This experience carried over to other groups with the added benefit that

105

she became an expert on cameras and photography and was looked to as an authority in this area wherever she went.

—— 181 · Ask for Help

Asking for help is taking a risk as you may be refused. This keeps many shy people from getting the help they need and the help that is available. Instead, they unnecessarily fumble along. Actually people are usually pleased to be asked to give advice or assistance as it makes them feel special and capable. Asking for help is good experience for a shy person, as it is taking a risk and reaching out and getting a positive response.

Conversely, offering help is a good experience for shy persons as they are generally enthusiastically accepted and they get a sense of their own importance.

Scott did not understand how to do the term paper assignment and was too shy to ask questions in class because he was afraid of appearing stupid. He did gather courage to ask a classmate. He learned that this person was also foggy about what to do, so together they approached the class brain who was able to explain it to them. By doing this Scott learned that he wasn't stupid. He helped a classmate find the information he needed too and he made the person who helped them feel good because she knew something she could pass on to them. Everybody ended up feeling better.

—— 182 · Share Yourself

If you think you are boring and no one would be interested in anything about you, you are wrong. It is not appropriate to share your life history with new acquaintances or with most people you know, but there are items of interest you can share that capture the human experience. Other people will identify with your statements, a conversation will take place, and they will feel closer to you.

Share your worry about getting evaluated or evaluating an employee.

If you aren't sensitive about age, talk about your joys or anxieties about growing older.

Talk about the experience of having a houseguest, or being one.

Complain about the telephone company, the post office, or the airlines, but not to employees of those companies.

Point out a slight phobia you have such as the common fears of public speaking or snakes.

Mention the challenge of living with a teenager.

Express your pet peeves such as standing in line, being put "on hold" on the telephone, or people who monopolize a conversation.

Lynn liked the person she was with, but didn't know how to make a connection with her. When she brought up what she was going through in trying to buy presents for the men in her family, Lynn's partner in conversation identified with her immediately. Their complaining led to mutual problem solving. A friendship developed.

——183 · Organize Activities

Shy people find it harder to manage themselves around people if they have to rely totally on their own resources. Thus, it is good to invite people to do things. Ask people to go to places or programs, or to participate in projects. This gives you an opportunity to have person-to-person contact without the pressure of having to be entertaining. It will help you develop your social skills in an enjoyable, nondemanding way. Request that your acquaintance accompany you to lunch or dinner or to a play, lecture, or sports event.

——184 · Practice, Practice, Practice

Doing a few of the recommended activities now and then is not going to do much to bring about expertise or increase your comfort level with people. Many suggestions are listed so you can find several approaches that you can use simultaneously. Practice every day. Talk to people while standing in lines. Purposely ask directions to find something while in a store. Stop and ask directions to a destination while driving. Make talking to people a daily priority. Soon it will become common practice.

You will notice it is second nature rather than a chore you have to make yourself do. When talking to others is a relaxed habit you know you are no longer shy.

——185 · Attack Your Areas of Shyness

You probably have more difficulty in some places, with some situations, and with some people. List the people who make you feel most shy. Analyze what they do that makes you feel shy. Work out a plan to compensate for that feeling when you are with them. Sit down, pull up an empty chair, and tell the imaginary person how you feel and what you plan to do about it. Switch chairs, pretend to be that person, and respond to yourself. Go back to your own chair and have the last word.

List places and situations that bring out your shy behaviors. Write out why you think these places and situations bring out your shyness. Close your eyes. Imagine yourself in these places and situations acting the way you would like to. Write down the behaviors and attitudes you visualized. Mentally practice the desired behaviors everyday for a week. The next time you are to be in a place or situation that makes you uncomfortable read your notes on the new behaviors and attitudes you visualized. Visualize them three more times, then go and use them.

——186 · Role-Play

Many public performers are shy people. They manage very well on the stage or screen as they are acting a role. You can do this too. Decide what role you want to play. Dress for the part. Plan your script. Rehearse. As you get into the role your stage-fright will disappear just as it does for actors and actresses. The role you picked is how you want to be. As you practice this role and find it rewarding, it will become you.

Stephanie saw herself as aloof and introspective. Her shy behavior prevented her from reaching out to others as she wanted to do. She wanted to be seen as the person she knew she was. She designed a part for herself to play based on a popular murder mystery writer she regularly watched on television. She saw her character as assertive and involved in helping people. She developed her character in her mind. She figured out what she, as that type of person, would say and do in certain situations in which she was going to be involved. She selected clothes to match her new persona. She had never had so much fun in her life. She was the only one who knew she was playing a part, but it worked. People did respond to the person she wanted to be and could act out. In places it was a bit rough, but she could rewrite those parts and adapt them to what she was like. Stephanie was thrilled to find that she could be the person she wanted to be. What started as an act became an integral part of her way to be.

187 · Keep Notes

Without a map you don't know where you are. The same holds true for the new you. Write down what works for you and what went wrong. As you accumulate information you will accumulate knowledge of how to handle practically every situation and personality you encounter. Even better, you will learn how to be happy in practically all circumstances and with almost all people.

The best way to manage note keeping is to get into a habit of doing it daily. Do not make long entries into your journal. Briefly jot down only what is important. How many people did you approach? What worked? Make a special notation of feelings of success. These self-addressed memorandums will be a reference for you and serve as a reminder of how far you have come as you continually improve.

188 · Know Any Good Jokes?

Some people can't tell the best joke in the world and make it funny. If you are one of those forget this quick fix. But a few funny stories, told well, are always appreciated. Humor is welcome in almost any setting. Collect jokes. Select short jokes with a surprising punch line. Keep away from controversial or questionable topics. Practice telling the joke until you get it right. Then look for a place to fit it in. You may start out your conversation with the fact that you have a good joke, tell it, and let the conversation roll. You have made your verbal entry into the social milieu. It is easy going from there. If you use joke

109

telling as a conversational ploy on a regular basis you may become known for this skill. A joke will be expected. That isn't bad. But be prepared.

——189 · Conversation Pieces

When Justin was walking through the mall with a dozen roses in his hand several people made unsolicited comments to him. He loved the attention, particularly from the girls. He responded and had a prolonged conversation with one fetching female. The roses were an attention getter that set him apart from the others strolling through the shopping center. Obviously he did not use the rose come-on daily, but he did learn the effectiveness of carrying a conversation piece with him when he wanted to greet and meet people.

When you feel shy you often feel exposed if you are out there alone and on your own. Take some object with you that is a converation opener such as a controversial or best-selling book. Walking a dog (where allowed) always brings friendly comments. People will talk to your dog and you can include yourself in the conversation.

Kristen wore a bottle of bubble-making formula around her neck for her first night on the cruise. These can be purchased at variety stores and are made to be worn in that fashion. She caused quite a stir when she deftly made a few harmless bubbles with her bubble wand. Her cruise mates enjoyed it and she enjoyed the attention.

Stephen took his binoculars with him to the beach and to other outdoor events. When he spotted something interesting he asked others if they wanted to look. He found several potential friends this way. It was easy to go from looking to talking about what they saw.

This is not to say you need to walk on stilts or wear funny hats, but there is nothing to prevent you from doing that either.

——190 · Ask Advice

The next time you need additional information do not look it up, ask someone. Discuss your dilemmas with friends, neighbors, relatives, or coworkers. If you can't make the ball go into the basket, ask someone who can. You don't know what kind of weed killer to use. Call up your acquaintances who garden and find out what they recommend. Questions do not have to be directed only to those you know well. Ask someone you would like to know better. People like it when they are approached because they know something others don't. Make use of this universal characteristic to reap the benefits of their knowledge, get to know more people, and practice overcoming the habits that keep you acting shy.

191 · Be Prepared for the Lull

Pauses in conversations are great as they allow another person to take a turn, but lulls are deadly. The silence booms. If you have something to offer at such a moment you will be a hero. Be prepared with a topic to throw in during the lull and rescue the situation. This may be the time to tell your joke, to comment on the news of the day, to ask for advice on some problem you have been having, or even to use a cliché about the weather. Others will pounce on any topic you suggest as an opportunity to get past the awkward silence. Be the one to save the moment.

192 · Don't Just Walk Away

Shy people may feel unimportant and think that their departure will go unnoticed. Do not believe it for a minute. Never just walk away. If you need or want to leave a group at a party, make your apologies and excuses. If you do not exhibit this common courtesy you will be seen as rude, not shy.

193 · Take Credit

All your social successes are the result of who you are and what you have done. They are not accidents. They are the direct result of your actions. Nothing would have happened if you did not make it happen. Take credit for everything you do. Don't give credit to others, the circumstances, luck, the weather, whatever. Credit yourself. You were there. You did it. Reward yourself. You did good so be good to yourself. What would be an appropriate, simple, and quick reward? Is it reading time, new clothes, a long-distance telephone call, sitting on the beach, sleeping late, a massage, a favorite food? Or is it points or money toward a delayed, but larger reward such as a trip, a major purchase, or time off from work?

Mildred never felt that she had anything to do with social situations that turned out well for her. She attributed it to the kindness or skill of others. She thought she was so ineffective that it surely was not because of anything she was able to do.

After Mildred set concrete goals for herself to overcome her shyness, she decided she would reward herself for every effort she made. When she talked with others, invited people out, or made telephone calls she rewarded herself. Because she rewarded herself she began to see that what she did changed what had happened to her so she was able to take credit. Even so, the rewards did not seem to be motivating her as much as she would have liked them to. She did not get a lift from her rewards, nor was she inspired to continue her work on her shyness because of the rewards she gave herself. Self-congratulations did more for her and were more satisfying. She phased out the reward program because knowing that she was the one factor that was making new good experiences possible was all the inspiration she needed.

Jay needed more. He was happy for his progress but wanted to make something special out of it to reinforce his positive behavior. Each time he accomplished his plans he put a marble in a jar. Soon he had a large jar of marbles and knew he was following through on his plans to help himself. He recognized he could give himself credit, but got no big thrill out of a jar full of marbles. Obviously Jay's reward for himself helped him recognize his success, but was meaningless as a reinforcer. A jar of marbles didn't do much to make him feel that he was getting something extra for himself. Jay had to change his reward to something he wanted and enjoyed. He changed marbles to quarters and when there was enough money he treated himself to a home-delivered pizza. The reward became a reinforcer.

112   There is more to taking credit than just making sure you give yourself credit. You must also take credit where credit is due in work, family, and social situations. Your idea is your idea. Although bragging is not recommended, neither is false modesty. Speak up for yourself if you solved the problem or gave the good suggestion.

In addition, do not put yourself down. On occasion it sounds endearing and humble to indicate how you are less than perfect and, thus, very human. But in the case of a shy person struggling for comfort in social situations, negatives are toxic. You have been cautioned previously in this book to help yourself think positively. Also help yourself speak positively. If you can't think of something good to say about yourself, talk about something else.

——194 · Don't Compare

To realize a quick fix you must not compare yourself to anyone else. There is not one person in the world who could not find someone else who is better looking, smarter, more agile, or more accomplished. As you go along make your comparison with where you were to where you are now. See your progress. See your success. Nothing succeeds like success.

——195 · Nobody Is Looking

Shy people are exceptionally self-conscious. Although they do little to bring attention to themselves, they feel people are looking at them and judging them. Do not believe this. People are generally too busy being involved with themselves to give anyone else much scrutiny. Remember this. When you are engaged in conversation with others they are thinking about their ideas, words, and deeds, not yours. You are not being evaluated. You are seen for how you present yourself. As a shy person you are probably seen as quiet, sincere, and pleasant. As you become more socially confident you will be seen as friendly, interesting, and nice. If you help people feel good about themselves, you can be sure they will feel good about you. You do this by listening to them, learning from them, agreeing with them, and giving them compliments. These are all things that are pretty easy for a shy person to do and are some of the commandments

113

for good human relations. Greeting; smiling; using the person's name; acting friendly, cordial, and interested; giving praise; showing interest, consideration, and a sense of humor; and lending a helping hand will guarantee your popularity. If you develop these social skills people will be looking at you with approval if, of course, they are looking at you at all.

——196 · Ask Open-ended Questions

Others will think you are a wonderful conversationalist if you get them talking and then listen. To get people talking ask open-ended questions. These are questions that require a longer answer than yes or no. Some examples of open-ended questions are:

1. What is it like to live in *(Alaska)*?
2. What restaurants in this area do you recommend and what is good about the food there?
3. Tell me about your *(dog)*.
4. What is it like to be a *(police officer)*?

As you listen to the answers to your question show interest and give encouragement by making listening sounds:

1. That so!
2. Wow!
3. Umm.
4. Yes.
5. Great!
6. Tell me more.
7. Really?
8. You're kidding.
9. Uh-huh.

When you are thanked for an entertaining time say thank you even though you know you did little of the talking. You do know you did the right thing socially.

——197 · Find Commonalities

People are intrigued by others who share their opinions, likes, and dislikes and other areas of commonalities. People from the same area, school, or background enjoy reminiscing about similar experiences and impressions.

When you say you feel the same way as the speaker, an immediate bond is formed. It is a compliment for a person to have his or her ideas or beliefs validated. Your opinions are of consequence. This does not mean you have to be a doormat to be liked and noticed. You may voice a difference and be respected. But when you find commonalities, use them to promote your sociability.

EASE PHYSICAL SYMPTOMS
Your physical symptoms of shyness can be managed so that they do not stand in your way. Here are some tips:

198 · **If you perspire excessively wear clothing that does not show stains. Buy strong antiperspirants and use them liberally.**

199 · **Take deep breaths if you feel a blush coming on. The blush will be circumvented as the breathing interrupts the blushing process.**

200 · **When your heart starts to pound, try any of the quick relaxation exercises in the anxiety section of this book.**

201 · **Overcome dry mouth by carrying a drink with you or suck on hard candies.**

202 · **Prevent an upset stomach by eating bland foods and using antacid tablets or liquids.**

—203 · Be aware of annoying nervous habits such as pulling your hair or clearing your throat. Consciously try to keep from doing them. Do something else to relieve tension. Carry a worry stone. Fiddle with any hand-held prop such as a camera, puzzle, handkerchief, or notebook. Take a sip of a drink or a bite of a cracker.

—204 · Collect Notable Mementos

You have had successes. You have had experiences you enjoyed. You have been given admiration. You have done good things. You proud of certain achievements. Make the effort to collect mementos from all those experiences and put them together in a scrapbook or box so you can see that you have made an impact and are a capable person. These might be the following:

        1. pay stubs
        2. raises

3. promotions
4. artwork
5. writings
6. invitations
7. diplomas
8. thank-you notes
9. photographs
10. crafts
11. letters and postcards
12. greeting cards
13. report cards
14. admission stubs

Don't be fussy. Add anything that makes you feel good.

LONG-TERM WORK

If you do some of the recommended quick-fix exercises you will be doing so well you will probably want to do more to develop your social side. Some suggestions are:

————205 · Take courses in assertiveness, speech, and in skills that involve contact with others such as dancing, bridge, and team sports.

————206 · Practice your speaking and social repartee using a tape recorder.

————207 · Watch how announcers and actors on television handle themselves and try some of the roles.

————208 · Get a make-over.

————209 · Work on your self-confidence.

Take a self-awareness course. Read self-help books. See the chapter on lack of self-confidence in this book. See also, Chapter 3 Stress, Chapter 1 Anxiety, and Chapter 2 Worry.

Chapter
FIVE

LACK OF
SELF-
CONFIDENCE

PEOPLE WHO APPEAR self-confident are admired. It is believed that those with self-confidence have it because they do what they do very well. They look as though they feel good about themselves. Although self-confident people are respected, cocky people and egotists are turn-offs. The latter are criticized for thinking too much of themselves. What is the fine line between being self-confident and being self-centered? Frankly, it is not a fine line. Whereas self-confident people have learned to accept themselves, the self-centered have not learned to accept themselves and overdo their sales pitch as they try to gain acceptance and approval from others. In these quick fixes you are not being told to become a conceited person focused only on your own self-interest. Instead you can use the methods outlined in this chapter to like yourself and live comfortably with the person you are. After all, who can you be but you? No one else has your particular arrangement of genes, chemicals, and experiences that make you the unique individual you are. You cannot be someone else. No one else can be you. Because you are you, you are a person of worth. You are worthy from the time you are born until the time you die. This does not change. There is no devaluation.

How do you know whether or not you have self-confidence? You are self-confident if you believe you are lovable and capable, and can do what has to be done to live successfully. If you are self-confident, you are trusting and trustworthy. You like others and you like yourself.

If you are not self-confident you have a tendency toward bragging, jealousy, possessiveness, and prejudice. You do what you do for the favor of others whether or not it conflicts with your own values. You may act a role because you do not feel the real you is good enough. You hate to admit mistakes, fear criticism, and are driven to succeed. You do not feel satisfaction in your success. You feel a failure even when you aren't. You feel unable to get what you want.

Confidence in yourself is one of the more important qualities for achieving happiness in life and adaptability to life.

If you are a person who feels severely lacking in confidence, it will take a while for you to recognize that the following quick fixes are working for you. Try them. You will find that they work. However, you may not feel more self-confident. This is because it takes time for feelings to catch up with facts. Although the exercises will be helpful for you, you may need therapy to convince yourself that the world is waiting for you and is ready to offer you good things.

If you are a person who generally feels good about yourself, the quick fixes in this section will help you feel even better.

• QUICK FIXES FOR LACK OF SELF- • • CONFIDENCE •

———210 • Define Your Problem

Even though you feel inferior you have areas of self-confidence. You may see yourself as a wipe-out in social settings, but you know you are a terrific parent. Conversely, the most self-confident individuals have times when they are plagued with feelings of inadequacy. Self-confidence may be no problem at work, but dealing with emotional situations may make a secure person feel that he or she is a failure.

Your problem may be situational. You feel competent sometimes and unable at others. Keep notes for a week. Have one column in which you enter feelings of mastery and another column to enter feelings of defeat.

If you have discovered areas in which you feel self-confident, figure out why that is so. What is there about the situation or your behavior that gives you confidence? Do you feel respected for your skill? Are you with people you know well and trust? Are you in charge?

Where are you when your confidence seems to run and hide, and you would like to do the same? Are you in a new situation? Is it when you are around authority? Do you see a common factor that is present each time you feel less than able?

Add to your two columns. Write what you do that gives you confidence and what doesn't. Can what you do in the feel-good column be applied to the not-feeling-very-good-at-all column? Do you have abilities that can be transferred or do you have to learn new skills?

Shirley's set of columns looked like this:

Doing Fine	Ugh
Fixing meals	Talking with the boss
Driving	Lunch with coworkers
Craft work	Getting the car inspected
Shopping	Working with the budget
Going to the beach	Meeting strangers
Telephoning friends	Defending personal point of
Taking college courses	view
Visiting with friends	Complaining about poor
Organizing responsibilities	service
and schedules.	

As Shirley surveyed the columns she saw her strengths in organizing, taking responsibility, pusuing intellectual as well as artistic endeavors, and being a good friend. She saw that she felt good in solitary activity. She believed this was a good indicator of personal security. When she acknowledged her intellectual, artistic, organizational, and socialization skills, she figured that she could apply these abilities to her work and personal business dealings. Knowing she had transferable proficiencies made her feel more confident. She set about seeing how she could make the best use of what she had.

Since she was confident with her friends, she wondered why she was not equally as able with her coworkers and strangers. She recollected that her friends were once strangers to her. Why was she comfortable with them? It was because she was herself with them. She decided she would work at being herself with her coworkers and with strangers. She would risk it. Acting a role was hard. If her friends accepted her the way she was, maybe she could expect others to do so too.

Shirley pondered. If shopping was no problem for her, why was taking care of complaints so difficult? She tried looking at following up on poor service as a form of shopping. This helped her transfer skills from what she liked to what she felt she had to do.

Shirley knew the budget was befuddling to her because she felt incompetent in mathematics. Since she liked college courses and getting good grades made her feel confident, she decided to take mathematics, bookkeeping, and accounting courses until she no longer felt a lack of confidence when dealing with numbers.

Shirley wondered why getting her car inspected bothered her when driving did not. At that point she decided that she felt good enough about herself and that feeling nervous about the inspection process was something she was not going to worry about, nor was she going to do it. She hired her neighbor's teenage daughter to do it for her.

─────211 · Help Others Develop Self-Confidence

It is harder to help yourself than it is to help someone else. To get a quick fix, find someone who lacks confidence and decide to help that person. It is easier to see what the other person needs to do to develop self-confidence than it is to see what you have to do. As you help him or her you will be helping yourself. How do you help? You help by offering encouragement. You help her or him open up and talk in a natural way. You listen and are interested and accepting. You never put the other person down. You may recognize that the individual you are helping has faults and weaknesses. You do not criticize or point them out. You see her or him as a valuable human being who, like everybody else, is not perfect. You help him or her develop in a positive way instead of focusing on the negatives.

Melissa was not a self-confident person. She recognized many of these same characteristics in Lauren. It was painful for her to see Lauren suffer just as she did. She knew how it felt. She also knew, from personal knowledge and observation, that Lauren had many reasons to feel confident but kept letting her feelings about herself get in the way. She did not speak up for herself. She was timid. No one realized what she could do. Even though Melissa had the same problems herself, she wanted Lauren to be free of the shackles of self-consciousness. Melissa set out to help her.

Melissa complimented Lauren on how she looked. She praised her for her special skills. She encouraged her to try out for a part in the play the local community theater was giving. She lauded her performance. She continued to emphasize all that Lauren did well and what she appreciated about her. She dismissed Lauren's complaints about herself, pointing out a positive quality whenever Lauren criticized herself. Lauren started noticing her successes. She began to feel better about herself and blossomed into a self-confident woman.

Melissa benefitted too. As she saw how her efforts were helping Lauren, she saw how to help herself. She put the same principles in effect for herself so she too was able to feel self-confident. She also felt powerful and clever that she had been able to help her friend.

———212 · Redefine Failure

Failure is a devastating word because it implies doing wrong, losing out, and being disgraced. Anything that dreadful is not among life's desired experiences. Since everyone fails, and does so fairly often, failure needs to be redefined so the experiences can be used for self-benefit. Do not endure misery. Use what happened to enhance your feeling of personal success. See failure as

1. a lesson
2. an experience

3. something that is past
4. interesting
5. a challenge
6. a new beginning

For example:

1. Failure as a lesson

Life is full of lessons, although a lot of them are overlooked. A failure, however, is hard to ignore, so welcome failure as it teaches you a strong lesson. What are some lessons to learn from your failures? The most important lessons are learning how not to do something or who not to do that something with. You can also look at failure as a way to fine-tune your approaches. Whatever you did, did not work. You now know that a different method will be better. Unless you learn where you were off-base you will not know how to make corrections.

Since failure is such a potent teacher, enjoy its benefits and hope that it happens early on so you can get wise sooner. Wouldn't you rather fail in your investment strategy after you lose $5000 than after you lose $50,000? Wouldn't you prefer that your marriage collapse three years before the children are born than three years after their arrival? Wouldn't you be relieved if you failed to get the airplane off the ground instead of being unable to land it?

William always wanted to be an actor. After playing many small parts he landed a major role in a play. He did as well as he could, but the critic's review was devastating to him. He felt a public failure. He did not want to face his peers, the audience, his friends, and relatives. What he really wanted to do was to disappear. He barely made it through the next three days. By the time he was getting tired of the pain, he noticed that everyone was treating him the same as they always had. Nothing seemed to be changing in his life so he worked up enough courage to reread the review. Since time had passed he was slightly more objective. William learned that the writer's evaluation of him was based on what she saw him capable of doing compared to what he was actually doing. The critic said the part was wrong for him. Now he was interested. There was a lesson to be learned here. Because he was handsome and sexy looking, William was frequently offered roles as the romantic hero and since he wanted to build his portfolio and needed the work, he took those roles. However, he preferred doing comedy and felt right playing comedic parts. He realized that he knew what was right for him and decided to pursue what he enjoyed and was good at. He stopped wasting his energy playing characters that were wrong for him. He learned a lesson that helped him channel his talent and develop it in a direction that brought him personal and professional rewards. Guess what happened to his self-confidence.

2. Failure as an experience

Is there something you have always wanted to do? Do you prevent yourself from having the experience because of fear of failure? If you keep yourself from taking risks, if you cripple yourself by limiting yourself, if you do not do what you want to do, your self-confidence suffers. You are giving yourself the message that you cannot do anything unless you can succeed in it or do it correctly the first time. This means that you can't try out anything you might like or become good at with practice. Try it. If it doesn't work out the first time you can readjust your technique and try it again. Or you can decide you never want to do it again as long as you live.

Laura always wanted to be on a talk show. When she got the opportunity she tried it. She was not particularly great but she knew she had given it a shot and did not have to spend her years wishing and wondering. Her self-confidence was not damaged as she viewed the experience as just that, an experience.

Thomas was upset when his girlfriend signed him up for mixed badminton doubles. Instead of backing out, he tried. He was not very good as he had never played before. She never asked him to play again, but it was an experience they never forgot. They reminisce about it after twenty years of marriage. Apparently Thomas saw his performance as an experience, not a failure. His girlfriend/wife perceived it that way too. Most of all she did not see Thomas as a failure. His self-confidence did not hinge on whether or not he played badminton well.

3. Failure as something that is past

When you fail at something it does not make you a failure for life. It does not even make you a failure at the time. It only

125

means that one effort was misdirected. When that one effort does not work out, you do not have to do the same thing in the same way again. You should feel good enough about yourself to realize that a mistake does not mean that you can do nothing right. A mistake means that you did that one thing incorrectly. And, as soon as you have done it, it is over, it is past. Plan for what is next. You are the person you have to live with. Forgive yourself for past failures whether or not anyone else does.

4. Failure as interesting

Some failures are calamities, most are not. Failures are part of what goes on in a lifetime of experiences. Put them in perspective as interesting events. You can make it more interesting if you analyze them for humor, pathos, and lessons to be learned.

5. Failure as a challenge

So it didn't work out this time. That can give you motivation to make it work the next time. You should see not getting it right the first or second time as steps toward success. The challenge is to move ahead after each setback. The saying is two steps forward, one step back. Build your self-confidence on the fact you tried and that the failure cannot stop you from trying again and doing better the next time. You are now smarter and more experienced.

6. Failure as a new beginning

Prisoners of war who have been tortured, and in the process revealed classified information, feel demoralized, not only because of their physical torment, but because of their feeling that they failed. To counteract this devastating reaction, a new approach was needed. Thus was born the bounce-back technique. Bounce back offers a new beginning. It means that the person recovers, moves on, and starts again from square one. The principle implies that extenuating circumstances caused the failure and that persons should forgive themselves and start all over again as though it did not happen. Prisoners of war did not see themselves as failures after they failed to keep military secrets when they used the bounce-back procedure. They had not lost their war. They had a setback in one battle. They did not have to maintain an attitude of defeat. They started over as though it had not happened.

You can do this with failure too. You can bounce back. You can start over.

Kelly had an off night. She could not hit. She could not run. She could not throw. She decided she was a public disgrace and should be off the baseball team. This frame of reference could have ruined her enjoyment of sports. She decided to see the episode as a glitch rather than a failure and start all over. She did. One game did not make her a failure for life. It was an event that inspired a new beginning.

──213 · Like Yourself

You may have found out by now that not everyone likes you. This is not because of how you look or act, or because of any logical reason. The people who like you probably don't have a logical reason for viewing you favorably either. The most popular and famous among us, elected officials, music and sports stars, and beauty queens, are not universally admired and loved. All are criticized. Those whom we don't like enjoy the love of some. Imprisoned murderers get married. Embezzlers, bullies, and put-down artists have friends and families who remain loyal to them.

Since being liked depends so much on factors over which you have little control, you are better off to control the one factor you can, which is how you feel about yourself. Of course, you can change to be more likable, but the changes should be made to meet your approval. Other people may not notice or care, nor will they understand. Take responsibility for doing what needs to be done so that you like you. Until you understand that self-confidence is internal and not dependent on externals, such as what you have and who you are with, the feeling of confidence will always elude you.

If this is a problem for you, get busy and determine what you like about yourself. If you aren't particularly fond of something about yourself, change it or accept it.

If you need to learn to like yourself do the following exercise.

    A. Make a list of twelve things you like about yourself. They could be:

1. kind to my dog
2. nice knees
3. wavy hair
4. reliable
5. seldom sick
6. keep appointments
7. compassionate toward others
8. good manners
9. good dresser
10. neat
11. clean
12. laugh a lot

B. Every day add three more items. These can be items that you add to the what I like about me list or something you did that day that you felt good about, something you enjoyed or accomplished, or a satisfying experience. For example:

13. Read good books.
14. Jamie admired my car today.
15. I was the first one at the meeting and got to talk informally with the boss.

Do this every day for three weeks. By that time your attitude will have changed to one that regards yourself highly. Save the list. Refer to it and add to it frequently.

——214 · It's Up to You

If you are waiting for something to happen to give you self-confidence consider yourself on permanent hold. You will find your life in limbo. Getting the promotion, marrying the right person, becoming famous, losing weight, or getting rich are all nice, but are not cures for lack of self-confidence. It is up to you to develop your own self-confidence. The good news is that you can do it. You can do it by affirming yourself. Two times every day give yourself six messages that are unambiguously positive. For example:

1. I look good.
2. I act good.

3. I have a terrific smile.
4. People like me.
5. People admire me.
6. I am capable.

You may want to throw in, "Every day, in every way, I am getting better and better."

Tailor your self-affirmations to what you want your self-image to be. Make sure they are totally positive. Do not slip in qualifiers such as most of the time, if I lose ten pounds, or if I could learn more. Also, they do not have to be statements that you initially believe. Remember that you are working to become self-confident. Consequently, you are unlikely to think that any six statements about yourself that are remarkably good can possibly be true. The point of this exercise is to get you to feel good about yourself and self-confident.

This exercise is insidiously effective. Since you probably will start feeling better in about ten days, the tendency is for you to slack off. Do not do it. Keep it up. Add to your affirmations. You can also change your affirmations to include other facets of your life and personality. Above all, do not stop.

Horace suffered from the impostor phenomenon. Although he looked good and acted and functioned well he could not believe that that was the real him. It was a facade. If people ever found out who he really was he knew he would be castigated and shunned. His world, which he was convinced was built on false premises, would fall apart.

Horace needed to realize his real worth to experience self-confidence. He was sure the qualities he exhibited to others were not truly his. He thought this because his parents had inadvertently given him that message. He had been compared to his older sister when he was growing up and he fell short. He did not walk, talk, or perform physically as soon or as well as she did. She got better grades in school and a better scholarship to college. He excelled in his own areas, and although these were noted, he measured himself by his sister's successes. His parents had not been aware that judging their second born by what their first born did made Horace feel he did not do well enough. Even though it was unintentional, the damage was

129

done. It was important for Horace to feed some positive affirmations into his memory bank. His six statements were

> I am the best.
> I am successful.
> I take good care of myself.
> I am highly regarded.
> People like me just the way I am.
> I can be myself.

Horace made these statements while looking in the mirror every night and every morning. Being an analytical person he really could not see how this could help him, but he did know that it made him feel better. So he kept it up and soon the positive affirmations infiltrated his being and he found himself feeling and acting with more self-confidence. He believed he had something other than a false front to offer his employers, family, and friends.

Since Horace felt more self-confident he was able to use the day's experiences in a more positive way. At the end of each day he noted all the good and interesting things that had happened to him. He wanted to acknowledge the reasons he had to feel good about himself and enjoy life now that he was developing a new outlook. He tried to list ten items every day. One day's tally looked like this:

1. Found a new way to go to work with less traffic.
2. Sally trusted me with a problem she wanted to discuss.
3. Guy asked me to have lunch with him.
4. I found a comfortable pair of shoes.
5. I stayed on my diet until I got home.
6. Heard a good joke I can retell.
7. No junk mail today.
8. My daughter smiled at me when I came home.
9. The neighbor mowed her lawn.
10. Loved the spring air.

These may seem ordinary, but from Horace's point of view they were exciting because he was open to experiencing the world in a new way. He gave himself credit for small successes and approval from others. He took pleasure in day-to-day activities that are easy to overlook. He came alive.

As Horace filled his mind with good thoughts about himself

and about life he became an optimistic person. He felt successful and began to see success as the likely outcome for all that
he did. Since he expected to succeed, he usually did succeed.

All this started with six short affirmations.

————215 · No Unfair Comparisons

We can ruin any good feelings about ourselves in the second
it takes to compare our weak points to someone else's strong
points.

You may be a good father while your friend Henry is in
charge of children's services for an entire state. If you lack self-
confidence, you might see yourself as a failure because you care
for one child while your acquaintance plans for hundreds.

You are not good at math. Susan is a whiz.

You are good at craft work, but that is nothing compared
with the fact that Velvet runs a department store.

Do you think these are ridiculous comparisons? I hope you
say yes, because they are. This is what people often do. They
compare capabilities that cannot be compared. Or they compare one skill with an altogether different skill, diminishing or
discounting their ability.

Rebecca was an expert labor negotiator, but she could go
into a black mood whenever she met someone who wrote well.
It always made her feel inadequate because she could not do
that.

Paul was a well-liked family man who was respected on his
job. He was an all-around good citizen. He always felt he was
less than others because he was not the head of any organization, was not a millionaire, and did not feel he excelled in any
area. Living a well-rounded, balanced life in which he made an
invaluable contribution to his family and friends did not bring
him self-confidence.

Rebecca and Paul had to learn that not everyone can do
everything. Their job was to acknowledge what they did well
and develop confidence in themselves because of that. There is
only so much time and energy. Rebecca concentrated on labor
negotiations. This took her energy and interest. This was
enough. She made her contribution. She was capable. She had

131

good reason to feel confident. Paul knew he was putting his effort into what was valuable to him. He knew that his family and community were his priorities. He needed to take pride that he was living in a way that gave his life meaning and satisfaction. Other paths may have taken him away from devoting his time and energy in these important areas.

Rebecca and Paul can be pleased to see people excel in areas where they do not. They should also be pleased to be able to do what they do well and confident in the choices they made.

———216 · Forgive Yourself

You have done things you regret, are ashamed of, and wish you could change. Everyone has. The reality is that the past is past. You cannot change anything that has already taken place. You may be able to make some amends through apologizing, discussing, or taking action that attempts to make up for what was not done. But you cannot undo. Even though you are disappointed in yourself, you must forgive yourself. This means that you acknowledge you did wrong, you learn from what you did, and decide not to do it again. Then you forgive yourself. Self-forgiveness is important because you have to live with yourself. Your self-confidence is compromised if you keep punishing yourself, feel guilty, or feel you are a bad person. Whatever you did or said, put it in the past, regret it, vow never to do it again, and let it go. When you do that and allow yourself to place your concentration on the parts of you you see as good and responsible, you will be able to feel self-confident. Here are the steps for forgiving yourself.

1. Isolate the problem behavior that makes you feel like a bad person.
2. Identify the feelings associated with that behavior. It may be shame, distress, fear, or grief. Allow yourself to feel those feelings.
3. Decide what, if anything, you can do about what you did. If you can do something, do it. Make amends if it is possible.
4. Figure out what you learned from the problem behavior. Did you learn anything that will make you a better per-

son today? All is not lost if you can profit in a way that enhances who you are now.

5. Recognize that the incidents are in the past. You have done everything you could possibly do. Decide to forgive yourself.

6. Forgive yourself.

You are not doing yourself or anyone else any good if you are morose about the past. You and those who care about you have to live in the present and have to live with who you are now. Get rid of the ghosts of the past. Let the past influence your behavior for the better, not drag you down with impotent contrition. Be proud of the person you have become. Be self-confident.

A few words of caution regarding amends are in order. To make yourself feel good is no reason to make adult children dependent on you if they should be developing into secure, responsible adults. You cannot make up for what you did not give them when they were children. You can apologize and strive for a good relationship with them and do what you can do to make life easier for them, but you must refrain from putting them in a position of dependency to appease your guilt.

Jeremy knew that his past alcoholism made his wife's and children's lives miserable. When he stopped drinking he was filled with remorse for his behavior. He had yelled at and insulted his family members. He has squandered money on his drinking that was needed for other expenses. He had ruined family functions with his drunken behavior. He had embarrassed his chidlren in front of their friends. He had been unreliable. He had lost jobs. In the end he lost his family. In the process of stopping drinking he became repentant over his past behavior. He figured that what he did was unforgivable. He felt he could not live with what he had done to the people he loved. He suffered from low self-esteem and punished himself for everything he did wrong in his past life.

No one could tell Jeremy that what he did as an alcoholic was all right. Many people could tell Jeremy that the person he had become as a recovering alcoholic was fine. But for Jeremy to enjoy his new directions he needed to learn to appreciate himself. To appreciate himself he had to acknowledge the past, grieve his actions, do what he could to help the people he hurt, learn from the experience, forgive himself, and move on. Jeremy faced the problem, went through his negative feelings about the alcoholic incidents, and set out to apologize to his family members and take the blame for what he did to them. He did not ask for forgiveness as he knew their forgiveness might not be forthcoming, and it was his forgiveness of himself that was the most important ingredient. After he did this he knew he had learned that he could never drink again, that he had an obligation to himself and others to act responsibly, and he forgave himself. This did not mean that he condoned what he did or stopped deploring it. It meant that he decided he had to and would live with the person he had been and had become. He felt confident in the fact that he turned his life around and confident in his ability to hold to new and better behaviors.

—217 · Dwell on Your Strengths

You have strengths and weaknesses. You have preferences and interests. Like all human beings you cannot be all things to all people because you cannot do all things. If you dwell on your weaknesses you will not develop self-confidence. If you appreciate your strengths you will.

Sean knew that his coordination and balance were terrific, but he did not enjoy sports and did not want to be a high-wire trapeze artist. He wanted to be an accountant. He liked to work by himself. He liked numbers. Unfortunately, he was not given to accuracy and frequently transposed numbers. He was unhappy because he could not do as he wanted. He considered himself a failure. He ignored his strengths and concentrated on his weaknesses. When Sean came around to accepting what he was good at and stopped moaning about what he couldn't do well enough, he put his skills to work. He became a very successful jewelry maker. He was able to work alone, creatively, and use his strengths.

Joyce grew up in a family that valued education over all. Joyce did not like school and did not do well because of her lack of interest and the pressure she felt from her family. She

did not perform well in tests as she was so nervous she couldn't think. Her grades were unspectacular.

Joyce enjoyed music. She didn't want to teach it; she wanted to perform. Her happiest moments where when she was on stage during plays and concerts. But she always felt this was frivolous as it was not what her family thought was valuable. She lacked confidence in herself because she did not develop in the direction her family wanted for her. Only when she recognized that her strengths did not coincide with her family's priorities, and that she owed it to herself to develop those strengths, did she become self-confident. She saw that she had every right to appreciate her achievements. She was not less than the rest of her family, she was just different from them.

Lester kept wanting to do better. He did not know what he wanted to do better at, he just knew that he felt he was not much good at anything. He emphasized everything he wasn't good at to encourage himself to do better. Unfortunately, since he was not able to do well in those areas he kept thinking he was an incapable person. What he did well he took for granted. One day Lester sat down to list all his shortcomings. They were as follows:

135

1. barely made it through school
2. not good at sports
3. not good in social situations
4. not physically attractive

Lester was lucky. As he was working on his list his wife came by and wrote out a strength list for him. It said:

1. good worker
2. good sense of humor
3. supportive of others
4. reliable and loyal

She suggested (rather forcibly, as she was sick and tired of Lester's attitude of defeat) that Lester pay attention to his attributes and work on them instead of always floundering around in areas in which he could not make much of an impact. To Lester's credit, he listened. He followed her advice. He felt more confidence in himself because he changed his attitude about himself.

Neil was brilliant. Neil was ambitious. Neil had been told that he was a boy wonder and would be the family's salvation. He took this script very seriously and expected to conform to the expectations of his family. However, he did not complete college, he was laid off his first job, and when he opened his own business it got off to a slow start. By the time his business was successful enough to support him and his family with money left over for savings, entertainment, and any extras he desired, he had become a very nervous person who felt he was not living up to his promise. He had to reprogram himself to see that he was meeting his own goals, making a contribution, and leading a good life. He looked at his strengths and what he was doing, rather than what his family expected of him. He recognized that he had every reason to feel self-confident.

——218 · Be Yourself

How, you may ask, can you be anybody but yourself? It's easy. You can pretend to be something you are not. This does not mean that you cannot improve or strive to develop in areas you have neglected. You can learn to be better or different by changing your attitudes and behaviors. But you cannot carry off an impersonation if that impersonation does not reflect who you are. The more comfortable you are with yourself the more comfortable other people will be with you and the more self-confident you will be.

For example:

You may be able to act the tough guy in a play, but you cannot carry this over to everyday life if this is not you. Others will see through it. If you cannot manage the tough guy role you may be able to stand up for your rights by supporting causes you believe in.

You may have a great deal of knowledge, but you are not expected to know everything. If you feel you must impress people with your erudition you will be known as a know-it-all.

You may admire those who are witty and humorous, but you may not be good at remembering or telling jokes. If you force it, it will fall flat. So you can't tell a joke. You can laugh and appreciate the humor of others.

Even though you may not be accepted as the one with the last word on every subject, you can be a contributor to every conversation.

Find out where you fit in and accept this as you. Work on what is possible. You have probably heard about not fitting round pegs into square holes. Only when you accept yourself can you progress and make the changes you want.

If you are not yourself it means that you believe you are unacceptable. It also means that you know you are an imposter. You will worry about being found out. The real you is fine. People cannot see your past and problems by looking at you. They see you as a kind, helpful person if you are a kind, helpful person. They see you as someone who does a good job if you do a good job. They see you as a happy person if you look as though you are having a good time.

Let's not confuse being yourself with being an unsociable bore. Being yourself does not mean that you never bathe, insult friends, eat without regard for any of the social graces, and wear ripped jeans to a formal banquet. Being yourself means that you function within the range of legal and acceptable behavior in the culture in which you live. The American way of life gives you great leeway. You may be drawn more to one life-

137

style than to another. Whatever your choice, in order to be self-confident you need to be yourself. You can change and improve the real you, but you cannot be someone else without becoming a parody of a person. There has to be a congruence between who you are and who you show to the world. If people accept the actor, you know they are not accepting you and you will not feel self-confident.

Living authentically cultivates self-confidence. If you can be yourself you will be more able to show and express your feelings, make your opinions known, be assertive, trust yourself and others, respect your rights and the rights of others, and know that approval of yourself is the only necessary approval.

Be yourself. Be your own hero. If you are yourself you never have to fear that people would not like you if they really knew you. Do not construe this to mean that you must disclose all your imperfections, dark secrets, and base thoughts. Take this as advice to act naturally and in keeping with the situation in which you find yourself. You may bare your soul to your psychotherapist, but you do not do this while attending a Sunday school class.

How do you go about being yourself?

1. Do not try to please everyone else. Insist on pleasing yourself.
2. Recognize that as a human being you are precious and have value and deserve the respect you give yourself.
3. Label yourself the way you want to be labeled, as long as it is a label that reflects your positive qualities.
4. Do not pretend to like, know, or have something you don't like, know, or have.
5. Give respect and love to those you care about. You will get respect and love in return. You may have risked rejection, but you will reap affection.
6. If you find it hard to be natural do it ten minutes at a time. Be authentic for that short period. It will feel good. Keep doing it at least ten minutes a day. Get as close to yourself as you can. Ask yourself if the situation is right for you. Question your true feelings. Do not act like you think you should. Find out how the real you is responding.

7. Accept other people for who they are and what they can mean to you. Forget your act. Pay attention to what the other person is like and whether or not this is someone you want in your life.
8. Accept all your feelings. You have the emotions of fear, sorrow, and anger just as you feel happy, proud, and strong. Do not try to shut off part of your emotional makeup or you will be shutting off part of you. Do not be afraid of letting positive and negative emotions show. This makes you a real person.
9. Do not try to be all things to all people. You have certain traits that incline you to certain actions and preferences. Follow these. If you are quiet and analytical you are not-likely to feel comfortable functioning in a noisy, action-oriented setting. Know this about yourself. Do not disparage yourself for being unable to do well in all arenas. Some people can make quick decisions, others have to be more thorough. Some want facts and the bottom line, others want details, reasons, feelings, and a review of the step-by-step process. Some people enjoy chaos, others need structure and routine. Which kind of person are you? Figure it out and realize you do not have to adapt readily to all people, systems, and settings. Be confident that your way is the right way for you.

——219 · Take Risks

Norman Cousins wrote, "People are never more insecure than when they become obsessed with their fears at the expense of their dreams." If you do not challenge yourself your world will become increasingly smaller. If your fears rule you, you will see yourself as weak. If you do not follow your dreams you will live a life of longing. If you continually protect yourself from your fears you will not develop self-confidence.

This is not a recommendation to become a daredevil. It is a recommendation to face your fears and take action to overcome them. Do your fears interfere with your life and what you want to do? If the answer is yes, think of the ways in which you are cramped by your fears and plan a procedure for overcoming them.

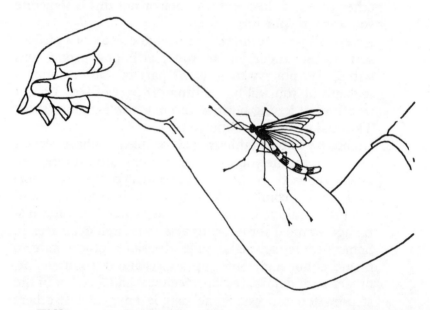

Tiffany was afraid of bugs. She did not want to go camping with her family and when she did she upset everybody. She was unhappy when they went without her. She was unhappy when she went with them. She tried blaming them for being inconsiderate, but she knew it was her own fear. She felt she was unfair to her family because she resented the fun they had. None of this was good for her self-confidence. She knew her job was to fight her fear. She decided to set up her own desensitization program as follows:

1. Tiffany read about bugs and looked at pictures of bugs.
2. Tiffany imagined bugs in the room with her.
   a. She visualized a bug.
   b. She imagined more bugs.
   c. She imagined different kinds of bugs.
   d. She pictured herself handling the bugs.
3. Tiffany went into the yard and looked at bugs. She touched a bug. She let a bug crawl on her. Nothing horrible happened.
4. Tiffany went on a camping trip and reassured herself

whenever she thought she saw or felt a bug. When Tiffany felt tense about bugs she told herself interesting facts she had read about them, she made herself breathe deeply and relax, and she reassured herself that she could hurt the bugs far more than any bug could hurt her.

5. Tiffany realized that bugs no longer held terror for her. Tiffany never learned to like bugs, but then, most people don't. She did enjoy camping with her family and felt better about herself.

Nicholas wanted a different job, but was terrified of job interviews. Rather than put himself on the line he stayed in a work situation he did not like. He hated being stuck and he hated himself for not doing something about it. Since Nicholas was preoccupied with his negative feelings about his job, his work deteriorated. After receiving several warnings he was fired. Now he had to look for a job. Necessity motivated him to tackle his fear. He read everything he could about how to prepare for a job interview. He learned that self-confidence was a major component that got people hired. This knowledge gave him a feeling of defeat, but he knew he could not give into this fear. He worked out a plan.

1. Nicholas wrote out his skills and interests. He memorized them.
2. Nicholas practiced with friends and family in front of a mirror with a tape recorder and a video camera.
3. Nicholas made a plan to sell his skills and experience to a prospective employer. He talked to two employers a day to let them know what he had to offer.
4. Nicholas felt self-confident when he went out for his interview. Since he was prepared he felt good about presenting himself.

Nicholas found a job he enjoyed. He was only sorry he hadn't conquered this fear before he was forced to do it.

Kimberly always wanted to be a lawyer but felt she was not smart enough to do the classwork. Her older brother had all the brains. She was never as good as he was. She had not done well in school. She had settled for a position as a legal secretary when she left high school. Nevertheless, her desire to be a lawyer burned within her. Her family got tired of hearing about the lawyers in her office and how she had always wanted to do that work. They told her to do something about her ambition or forget about it. But she always felt afraid to take the risk. When she reached fifty years of age she speculated on how she had never been able to do what she wanted to do and it was too bad she was not smart enough to pursue her dream. At that point a paralegal came to work in her office. She learned that paralegal classes met at night, were made up of adults, and could be taken one at a time. This gave Kimberly the incentive she needed to risk going to school. She went, found she was able to do the work, dropped out of paralegal school, and enrolled in courses that led to her law degree. Like everyone who finally takes a risk to achieve, she regretted that she had not made the move long ago. Kimberly made a happy, self-confident attorney.

220 · Develop a Support System

Obviously a person can maintain self-confidence while working and living alone. Writers, scientists, artists, and hostages spend hours in solitary because of what they do or what is thrust upon them. They do not develop low self-esteem because they do not get constant feedback about their accomplishments. But even people who are alone either because of their work or situation keep up their morale because of supportive relationships. They stay strong and able because of thoughts of the people they know who care.

You will build self-confidence if you strengthen family ties and keep strong friendships. This cannot be done passively. This takes telephone calls, thoughtful gestures, visits, and mutual experiences. Build on what you have. Give support to get support. Know who you can count on, and for what. No one person can be all that you need. Each friend and family member can make a contribution to your well-being and your self-confidence.

Kyle's mother gave him a feeling of security. His girlfriend made him feel good about himself because of her totally biased admiration. His friend Jeffrey helped him feel like a great conversationalist because of the long and interesting talks they had. The neighbor, Lisa, strengthened his confidence because of her compliments about his skill as a landscaper. Kyle appreciated his support people and gave to them in return.

Katie was frequently irritated with her friend Mary who was always late and sometimes forgot appointments. She often questioned if she really needed this. However, she knew that being tardy and sometimes irresponsible was Mary's problem and the behavior was not directed at her. She valued the fact that Mary always encouraged her in what she wanted to do. She chose to work at keeping Mary her friend in spite of irritations. Mary was good for Katie's self-confidence in one important area.

———221 · Don't Blame Others

Blaming others for something you have done wrong or a mistake you have made, instead of taking self-responsibility is an unappealing trait, a futile exercise, and evidence that you need to work on your self-confidence.

Taking the blame yourself brings you many benefits.

1. You can learn from the mistake.

If you do not take responsibility for your goofs you never have the opportunity to learn and to grow and to prevent the same or a similar incident from happening again. If you consistently blame others for everything that goes wrong, you will never develop personal control or responsibility.

2. You do not make others defensive.

If you blame others they will try to defend themselves. In defending themselves they will get defensive. In their defensiveness they will counterattack. People who are unjustly blamed will make it clear that they do not like it and that they do not like you for doing it.

3. You will see you are big enough to accept responsibility.

People who take responsibility are admired. Taking responsibility for mistakes is seen as integrity. You will be proud of your ability to accept the responsibility. In this way you can look good in a bad situation.

143

4. Accepting blame shows that you know that making a mistake does not make you a failure.

Since everyone makes mistakes, you have no reason to condemn yourself for making one. You can admit the mistake without admitting there is anything wrong with you.

5. You take the blame and you take control.

If you take responsibility for what went wrong it gives you the control to fix it and make it right. You can identify the problem and work for what will improve the situation.

6. Taking the blame dispels anger and resentment.

Denial of fault when the fault is clearly yours will bring anger and resentment down upon you. If you accept the blame the anger and resentment are defused.

7. Taking the blame brings respect and possible forgiveness.

People who admit mistakes, even when it is hard to do, are respected by others for their courageous stance. The admission may also bring forgiveness. It is hard to forgive someone who insists that he or she did nothing wrong. It is easy to forgive someone who accepts responsibility for what happened.

For one week keep a record of each time you try to cover up a mistake or resist trying something because you fear making a mistake. At the end of the week you will know if this is a problem for you and a threat to your self-confidence.

Do not take the blame for something you did not do in order to appear noble. But face up to your responsibilities and you will feel responsible and self-confident.

———222 · Be Realistic

It is good to dream. It is helpful to expect and plan for success. But you will experience disappointment and frustration if your expectations are unrealistic. Planning and communication will keep your self-confidence intact. Idealistic projection will result in feelings of being thwarted.

Stacy had big plans for the conference she and several of her coworkers were to attend. She expected that they would all "chum around," eat in exotic restaurants, and compile a report that would impress those who did not attend. However, she did not discuss her scheme with any of those who attended with her. When the group arrived at the conference setting one of them looked up old friends she had met at previous conferences, another had relatives in the city, and a third brought along work she had to complete during the time she was away. Stacy was left with no one to keep her company, and none of her coworkers was the least bit interested in preparing a presentation on what each learned at the conference. Extra, unrequired work was not on their program. Stacy felt rejected and her self-confidence suffered. This could have been avoided if she had prepared her agenda with her coworkers. She would have known what to expect.

——223 · Depend on Yourself

Humans are social beings. Support from others is necessary, but should not be the sole source of your self-confidence. Your major security is—guess who—you! The only person who has your interests in mind is you. The only person you can always depend on is you. The one person who is always on your side is you.

How do you learn to rely on yourself? You start by going places alone. You will find there is a freedom in doing this that you can never achieve when you are dependent on others for all your activities. Your schedule can be arranged to suit you. You can spend time at what you enjoy. You can eat, rest, or overexert whenever you want. You may prefer to have others accompany you, but relying on yourself for your own entertainment offers definite advantages and sets you free to do what you want to do.

Kevin loved to go out in his boat, but could never gather up people to go with him when he wanted to go. One particularly lovely day he went out alone. It was wonderful to have only himself to think about. He found that he was perfectly good company. He never felt frustrated again when he could not enlist a boating companion.

After Julie became a widow she had a lot of problems with her self-confidence as she was not accustomed to thinking in terms of one person. She also found that her married friends did not invite her out for evening events. She missed plays, concerts, and dinners at restaurants. When she could not find like-minded friends who wanted to pursue these activities as much as she did she bought a season ticket to the dinner theater. This worked out well for her as she had dining companions who were seated at her table. She felt more self-confident as she found herself functioning comfortably and making friends with people she had never met before. She went from this successful experience to traveling with a tour group to independent excursions whenever she felt like it. Her self-confidence was on an upswing.

——224 · Rewrite History

Your self-confidence is at a low ebb after you have been rejected, abandoned, fired, publicly embarrassed, physically hurt, or handicapped, and as a result of abuse or neglect in your childhood, or a shameful past. This is a natural and expected consequence of such events. Since you are a product of what happens to you, you cannot deny any of the unwanted occurrences. They happened. You survived, but you are wounded. Your job is not to ignore your past and pretend it did not happen, but to break away from the negative aspects by looking at what you learned and how you developed skills or positive character traits because of what happened to you. You can rewrite your history to dramatize the good results. This does not diminish the horrors or negate the negatives. It does give you an opportunity to recognize that out of the bad came some good and that good is in you. You will elevate your self-confidence.

Jill's boyfriend did not want to continue their relationship. He became involved with another woman. Jill was devastated. She felt she had done something wrong and would never be able to attract another man who would admire her. Why couldn't she hold on to a man? What was wrong with her? By the time Jill moved from despair to anger she had also moved to the fact that holding on to a relationship for the sake of a relationship was not a good move on her part. She strengthened herself when she reevaluated what she had been through on the basis of what she wanted in a mate. She saw this romance as a good example of what not to do in the future. No longer would she give all without getting. No longer would she accept only what a suitor had to offer if it wasn't what she wanted. She saw the rejection as an experience that helped her define what she wanted in a relationship. Knowing more precisely what she wanted made her feel self-confident when she entered into other male-female associations.

Mark was adopted when he was three years old. He knew his adoptive parents as his real parents and appreciated the love and care they gave him. Nevertheless, there lurked within him the idea that there must be something wrong with him if he was abandoned by his biological parents. Only when he rewrote that scenario and saw that he must have been so special that his parents let him go because they wanted the best for him, did his self-confidence emerge.

When Natalie was a teenager she was fired from a fast-food restaurant for goofing off. Since this had not happened to her friends, she felt she was a real loser. She carried the fear of losing a job with her into all her employment situations. When she was able to look at the experience through adult eyes, she saw that the incident had made her a better, more loyal, and conscientious worker. Because of this there was little danger of her losing her current job. This helped her improve her self-confidence.

Timothy's mother, a manic-depressive, came to his elementary school one day and made a scene in his classroom. This was the last straw for him. She had flirted with his friends, intruded in his activities, and told outrageous lies when she was in her manic state. Timothy was mortified and angry, then felt guilty about rejecting his mother. He managed the difficult situation by being secretive, avoiding home as much as possible, and leaving for good at the first opportunity. He always felt he would be a different person if he could have had the home life he imagined his friends had. When he took a less emotional look at his life he learned he had developed independence and self-reliance at an early age and that these skills had served him well through his life. He did not get the protection he craved, but he did get a self-sufficiency that he might not have had he had what he wanted. This gave him self-confidence.

147

At age twelve Shannon had an accident on the parallel bars during gym glass. She became confined to a wheelchair. She was grief-stricken and bitter. Since she could not physically do what her friends could do she fixated on this and her confidence dwindled. She was thirty-two years old before she discovered that everybody seemed to be less than adequate in some area of their lives. She knew people who were not very bright, who could never get organized, who had deficits in vision or hearing, and who had unattractive personalities. It was as this point that she saw that although she lost out in physical ability, she compensated for it by working hard to develop her mind and her personality. Because of this she did well in school, had many friends, and worked at a job she thoroughly enjoyed, in a field where she was considered an expert. At age thirty-two Shannon became a whole person. She gave up the bitterness that had ruled her life. She saw her development and success as congruent with what she wanted for herself. She saw every reason to feel the self-confidence that had previously eluded her.

Richard had been sexually abused by an older male cousin who also abused him with threats and demeaning taunts. Richard blocked out this traumatic part of his life, but was often depressed, and anxious, and had poor self-esteem. When memories of the abuse started to return he was devastated with negative feelings about himself and his past. It took therapy for Richard to discover that as bad as the experience had been, it had apparently unconsciously motivated him to help abused, abandoned, neglected, and troubled children. He was known for his skill in working with them and his advocacy on their behalf. Although Richard had to struggle to work through his feelings about his abuse, he did see the good that he did because of his experience. He felt self-confident in his work and was glad that he had channeled his hurts in such a constructive way.

———225 · Think Self-confidence

Olympic contenders and other competitive athletes have learned the value of self-confidence. At the level at which the best of the best compete it is often self-confidence that is the determining factor. The athletes with self-confidence who can perform without losing their focus because of precompetitive anxiety are the ones who win. To gain a winning attitude mental preparation is essential. Winning athletes use imagery and visualization (see the section on anxiety), stress management (see Chapter 3 Stress), and self-confidence. Olympic contenders must remove self-doubt and replace it with self-confidence. They cancel self-doubts and concentrate on successes and what they do well. They remind themselves of what they are capable of doing and how far they have come. They focus on the job, not on extraneous details.

Think self-confidence. Do not think about the man sleeping in the third row, how you are going to explain mistakes to your employer, whether or not you got a good haircut, or if it is going to rain all day. Take your nervous tension and channel it into what you are doing. If you are totally focused you will not be fretting about unrelated problems and you will perform in a self-confident manner.

Tara used her driving time to think self-confidence. She made a tape that psyched her into a state of self-esteem. Over the background of cheerful, relaxing music she inserted self-confident messages every minute. Some of these messages were:

You are competent.

You are able.

You are wonderful.

People admire you.

You do a great job.

You feel and act terrific.

You are especially good at *(selling, speaking, being a friend)*.

Tara tried it two ways. She made one tape saying "I am" and another saying "you are." For her, the "you are" tape worked the best. Tara found that her own voice helped her. She had her sister make a tape, but this did not do it for her. Often your own voice is the best for you, but you may be the one who finds another person's voice more believable.

——226 · Do Something Well

You do not have to excel in anything to enjoy self-confidence, but it helps.

Howard found doing a good job self-satisfying. The knowledge that he did so was a major compensation for the work done. This gave him self-confidence and an eagerness to be in the place where he felt good about what he did and about himself.

Joan was a changed child after she took karate lessons. She had previously been quiet and she was frequently tormented by the class bully. Knowing karate changed the way she handled herself and the way others regarded her. She developed self-confidence.

Jonathan was weird. He acted weird. He thought of himself as weird. However, he discovered he had a brain, and a good one. His self-confidence emerged after he enrolled in college and brought home superior grades. He soon had a reputation for being a whiz at his classwork and loved the attention he got for his knowledge. He had an aura of self-confidence. He still was weird, but now he was labeled as an eccentric. He was called a brilliant eccentric.

—————227 · One Day Doesn't Make a Summer

There is no always. There are no nevers. I never do anything right and I always make a mess of things are not only defeatist attitudes, they are wrong. Your inability to balance your checkbook without transposing numbers does not mean that you should never be trusted with money or that you always foul up. An unsuccessful occurrence or action is not an indication of a pattern of failure. One mistake in a long-term project does not make the project, or you, inadequate. If you were not a smash at the last party you attended that is not a sign that you should never attend another. Do not dwell on the fact that you could not answer question number seventy-three. Concentrate on the fact that you answered ninety-nine other questions.

Put a thick rubber band around your wrist. Every time you let one negative thought ruin what was otherwise positive, snap the band on your arm—hard.

—————228 · Appreciate Your Quirks

You have learned to appreciate all your fine qualities. You have, haven't you? You are self-confident. But you aren't perfect? That does seem to be a problem for all of us. Perhaps you need to accept yourself, blemishes and all. See your imperfections as endearing, enjoyable, human and part of the package that is you. Perhaps you could work harder to be more perfect, but you may not want to. It may not be worth the effort to learn to wash clothes the way your grandmother did or keep your garage as neat as your neighbor's.

Maybe you cannot remember names. Maybe you get lost coming home from work, and cannot put a nail in the wall without causing a major disaster. These are not problems. These are not reasons to challenge your self-confidence. These are parts of the you that has enough reasons to feel good about yourself. You can incorporate what you do not do well into your self-image. Don't be so hard on yourself.

229 • Take Care of Your Needs

Nobody really knows what you need. Although there may be many people who think they know, even your closest or most objective friend cannot identify your needs for you. This statement of fact should be your clue to the understanding that only you can know what you need and can go about fulfilling your needs. If you expect others to identify your needs and take care of you, you will have a long, frustrating wait. You will miss out in building your self-confidence. If you let others decide what is right for you, you will live a life of disappointment and wonder why you are never happy.

Jana was resentful of her husband. She wanted him to make her happy and he did not. He did not know this responsibility had been assigned him by his wife. As Jana allowed herself to feel neglected, she felt more powerless and less self-confident.

Karl knew he craved recognition. He expected it to be provided to him. Of course, it wasn't, or the recognition wasn't for the reason Karl wanted it or in the way he wanted.

Jana had to learn that she could make herself happy. Karl had to learn that he could give himself all the recognition he wanted. This is the road to independence, self-esteem, and self-confidence. Jana and Karl could change and feel their own power in making the change.

151

————230 · Please Yourself

If you do what you like to do in the way you like to do it, whenever that is possible for you, you will be doing what you are good at. You will be able to achieve more because you are doing what you like and will be willing to put more into it. This sounds like the roadway to self-confidence to me. Doing what you like helps you feel good. When you feel good you will put more time into it and you will succeed. If you succeed you will feel self-confident. And this starts with pleasing yourself.

Harriet enjoyed bowling. Because she liked it she joined a bowling league, even though she was not a topnotch bowler. As she practiced she got better. As she improved she could see her progress. She contributed to the team's success and soon felt confident of her skill and herself.

————231 · It Isn't All or Nothing

When everything seems to be falling apart, it probably is not falling apart in every area of your life. You may be having problems at work, but your friends continue to enjoy your company. You may not be able to get the house painted, but your paperwork is in order. Note your victories. Note what is going well. Feel confident that you are managing some areas of your life very well.

Ira was devoted to his children. When his wife left him, taking their son and daughter with her, he felt a total failure. His self-confidence hit an all-time low. It took effort, but he did notice that he continued to be a good elevator repairman and he was still winning the sailboat races in which he participated. He felt sad, but his self-confidence remained intact.

————232 · Allow for Differences

Not everyone thinks alike, likes the same things, or reacts the same to the same stimulus. Remember this if your self-confidence is shaken by people who disagree with you, do not like what you like, and have different feelings about the same event.

That does not mean that you are wrong and they are right or vice versa. It only indicates that you have different preferences.

In the same vein, you can dismiss people who appear to disagree with your ideas or actions. They have views that differ from yours, that's all. You do not have to see their disagreements as rejections or criticisms. Allow yourself your opinions. Stay self-confident.

This, like many of the other quick fixes, is truly quick. Instead of taking offense, take it as a different idea. You will feel instant relief and a surge in self-confidence if you do this. If you do it habitually, self-confidence will be a habit.

—233 · Don't Be Overprotective

Your ego is not as fragile as you may imagine it to be. It can be hurt, but there is no reason for damage to your ego to be permanent. Do not protect your ego so much that you keep yourself from trying new things, speaking out, or getting emotionally involved. If what you do does not work out, you are not hurt irreparably. If you shut yourself off to keep from getting hurt you shut yourself off from experiences and emotions that will cause you to lead only half a life. This is not good for your self-confidence as you know that you are so frail you cannot allow yourself to take a chance by doing something you might like to do. You will feel better about yourself if you express your real feelings, go to the meeting even if you have to go alone, and tell someone you love him or her. You will get over it if all does not go as planned and you will like yourself better for having tried.

—234 · Be Your Own Parent

Be the parent you always wanted to have. That is how you can learn to be the self-confident person you want to be. What does the ideal parent do? The parent does the following:
1. gives unconditional love
2. gives praise and encouragement
3. sets rules

153

    4. teaches skills

    5. helps in the socialization process

You can be your own parent until you develop a reputation with yourself that meets your approval.

    1. Give yourself unconditional love.

You may not like some of the things you do or some things about yourself, but you can still love yourself, no matter what. You love other imperfect people. Give yourself the same regard. Loving yourself does not make you narcissistic or vain. It makes you comfortable with yourself and self-confident. You are the one person in your life you have to live with. Do right by you. Enjoy your constant company.

    2. Give yourself praise and encouragement.

When you do something you like, let yourself know it. Reinforce doing well so it will stick in your consciousness and you can do what you approve of again and again so your self-respect continues at a high level and increases to a solid feeling of self-confidence.

    3. Set rules.

You know by now that certain behaviors or actions get you into trouble and make you feel bad. Set rules to curb these self-destructive deeds. Just as your parents warned you to look both ways before crossing the street, and the rule became second nature to you, so can your own rules instill in you a healthy and self-confident life.

Rules need not be "do not" rules such as do not be late for work and do not abuse alcohol. They can be "do" rules such as do take time for yourself, do play with the children, and do indulge in a pleasant exercise regularly.

    4. Teach yourself skills.

Your parents taught you to dress yourself and instructed you in other self-care skills that helped create the independent person you are today. If you feel a lack of self-confidence because of what you cannot do it is possible for you to learn. Teach yourself through self-help and how-to books. Learn through watching others and by taking instructional courses. Do not say that you would feel better if you knew how to drive, cook, set the

154

table for a formal dinner, or train your dog. Read books, ask others, take classes. Be able. Be independent. Be self-confident.

5. Learn social skills.

Many of the rules of social interaction are based on showing consideration, kindness, and interest in others. If you are unsure, and consequently do not have confidence in yourself, you can teach yourself. Read books on etiquette. Watch others. Do not be afraid to ask for guidance. Your desire to do the right thing will charm others. But you won't go wrong if you base your actions on concern for the feelings of others. In the end you will be pleased with yourself and will feel self-confident because you will feel more at ease in social situations.

———235 · Be Alert

Be alert to opportunities. Be aware of what is going on around you. Do not color your observations with fantasy.

1. Be alert to opportunities.

Forget that ignorance is bliss. Ignorance is ignorance. If you are alert to opportunities you will see what others miss. If you are not bogged down in your past you can be alert to the present and what the future may bring. Know your priorities and be alert to opportunities that fit with your values.

Iris wanted a committed relationship with a man. However, her lack of self-confidence caused her to miss many opportunities. She had to have a man fall into her lap before she was alert to the fact that there was someone available who might be right for her. When she learned to be alert to all the men in her environment, her opportunities increased, as did her confidence. She noticed more men. She talked with more men. She had more dates. She is still looking, but feels good about herself.

2. Be aware of what is going on around you.

Do not be the last one to know the company is closing, your neighbor is sick, prices are going down, or the rules are being revised. As you focus on the actions, viewpoints, and perspectives of others, you will see the big picture and be able to take action in a positive way. You will feel self-confident as you base

155

your decisions on observations you have made because you could look around you. You did not spend all your time monitoring your own feelings and the impact you were having on others.

3. Do not color your observations with fantasy.

When you are unrealistic about yourself, you are unrealistic about others. People in bad marriages often see any couple that is together as having an A-1 marriage. Nothing could be further from the truth. Unhappy people judge anyone who looks happy and carefree to be problem-free. Those who do not have what they want assume those that have it (money, health, family) have everything they want. If you think this way, you need a more accurate perspective. Everybody has limitations, disappointments, and hang-ups. If others appear to be handling their problems, let that give you hope and self-confidence. They may perceive *you* as a problem-free person.

Deal with reality. It is OK to dream, but it is not OK to lie to yourself or base your ideas on false premises. When Art Linkletter was speaking at the University of Nebraska in 1992 he said, "Things turn out best for the people who make the best of the way things turn out."

236 · Know When You Succeed

If you are not a self-confident person, there is a danger that you will not notice your successes, or will feel that one success is not enough, and continually strive to do more, never achieving self-satisfaction and self-confidence.

How do you know when you have succeeded? You know if you have reached your goal if you set a goal.

If your goal is to finish school, you can feel good about yourself when you do.

If your goal is to give a party your confidence in your success is warranted when you do.

Set realistic goals and declare your self-satisfaction when you reach them.

You know you have succeeded when you concentrate on your priorities.

If your priority is work you have succeeded each time you achieve on the job.

If your priority is a good family life, you can be happy when your home life is stable and rewarding.

If your priority is your religion and your successes are in business you will not be satisfied and confident until you put time and energy into your priority.

Results of a study completed by the Gallup Organization showed that people who equated success with happiness, peace of mind, and a good family life felt better about themselves than those who placed more weight on material things and success at work. This is why it is important to set goals that coincide with your priorities if you are to achieve self-confidence. If family life makes you happy and you spend all your time at the office you will not have a sense of good self-esteem. Know what success means to you, know when you have successes, and feel confident in your success.

——237 · Do Not Be Critical

You owe it to yourself not to be overly critical of yourself and others. Events won't go right. People won't do right. Mistakes will occur, and you will make some of them. A live-and-let-live attitude will bring you more peace of mind than an ever-vigilant posture of nitpicking. Do not let it bother you when people do really stupid things. They probably do not have an exclusive on stupidity. Putting others down to bring yourself up will not make you feel more self-confident. What will make you feel more self-confident and less annoyed is being able to take blunders in stride.

At his grandson's wedding all Phillip could talk about was the fact that the wedding had started one-half hour late.

Because Holly did not get the seat she wanted at the play, she felt righteously angry and complained the entire time.

Holly and Phillip would have enjoyed themselves more and garnered more respect from others if they had ignored the trivial mishaps they emphasized. They would have felt better

157

about themselves for being able to make the best of the situation.

———238 · List What You Want

What qualities do you see in self-confident people? List them. Then dissect something from your life that indicates that you have experienced that quality. For example:

Accountable
1. Always say when I'll be home or call when I'm delayed.
2. Pay my income tax on time.

Important
1. I am important to my bridge club. They need a substitute if I'm not there.
2. I am important to my children. They need me.

Interesting
1. My mother likes to hear about what I am doing.
2. My last trip outside the country provided me with many interesting anecdotes.

Valuable
1. I'm the only me there is.
2. People depend on me to do my job.

Needed
1. If I didn't set the alarm clock, no one would.
2. I'm the only one who remembers to walk the dog.

Independent
1. I change my own flat tires.
2. I can support myself.

Competent
1. I can cook anything I need or want.
2. I know how to get around in the city.
3. I know where to go to get the information and help I need.

Responsible
1. I go to work every day.
2. I complete tasks when I start them.

You will be able to find evidence of all these characteristics in yourself. List everything you think a self-confident person would have. Then list the evidence that these qualities are present in you. Some areas may need more improvement or more consistency. You can work on those as you build on the qualities that are already a part of you.

• IT'S NOT OVER 'TIL IT'S OVER •

The corollary to it's not over 'til it's over is it's never too late. Live your life each day. Do not set arbitrary milestone marks such as, "I'm (thirty, forty, fifty, sixty, seventy, eighty) and it's too late for me to do anything about this now." Self-confidence is yours at any age and has been achieved in every decade of life. You can grow to the last days of your life. In fact, as your experiences and perspectives increase, so do your opportunities. At a later age you can see more successes and satisfactions. A quick fix is yours whenever you decide the time is right.

See Chapter 4 Shyness, for further exercises to help you feel confident in social situations. Look at the anxiety section of this book for relaxation exercises. Consult the section on worry to learn positive self-talk.

JEALOUSY

JEALOUSY AND ENVY are two words that are often used interchangeably. Both have negative connotations and involve uncomfortable emotions. They can inspire you to do better and achieve more, but better and more do not always banish jealousy and envy.

Although jealousy and envy imply unhappiness with yourself in relationship to others, they do have different meanings. Jealousy is defined as an untrusting fear or suspicion of another. If you are jealous you are afraid that the person you admire likes someone else better than you.

You are envious if you feel discontent at the good fortune of others. You want their possessions, achievements, and activities for yourself.

Jealousy and envy are quite common. You may want someone to appreciate you more or you may want something someone else has. Even though you have these covetous feelings, it does not mean that you cannot be happy for another person's good luck.

Excessive jealousy and envy are commonly seen as symptoms of poor self-esteem. If you have problems in this area, see the chapter on self-confidence. When you feel better about yourself you will not feel the pangs of jealousy and envy as acutely.

• SYMPTOMS •

If you are jealous you want to know that there is no doubt that the person you love, loves only you. This is not a bad aspect of jealousy. It is a normal desire. If your jealousy is out of hand you are suspicious of your loved one's actions, thoughts, and feelings. Because of this you question what the person is doing, check into the person's activities, and need constant acknowledgment that you are number one. You end up unable to enjoy or believe that the person really likes you best. You see disloyalty in all that he or she does. You end up being distrustful, accusatory, controlling, and impossible to live with. You end up losing that which you most wanted to keep.

Nathan loved his wife's attractive personality. Others did too. People were drawn to her. Nathan would have liked to have had all of her attention for himself. He was jealous that she shared so much of herself with other people. He handled this by being more attentive and thoughtful. By being a more likable person he was more appealing to his wife. She voluntarily sought his company. Nathan used his feelings of jealousy constructively. He knew what he wanted and worked at getting it by improving himself.

Zachary also loved his wife. She thought his all-consuming interest in her was very special during their courtship period. Her friends were envious of all the attention Zachary had given her at that time. It was nice to have someone care that much. But the feeling of being special soon turned to a feeling of being trapped when Zachary wanted to know everything she had done all day. She found he was upset when she talked with her male next-door neighbor, negotiated a special cut of meat with the male butcher, and got a busy signal when he tried to call home during the day. He refused to let her visit her family without him, criticized her wardrobe as he thought it was too sexy, and insisted that she quit work after she mentioned that she had had lunch with some of her coworkers, one of whom was a male.

Zachary's jealousy drove his wife out of his life. What had seemed attentive to her when they first met, now was recognized as obsessive.

Nathan had his jealousy well in control. He might profit from some quick fixes he could use whenever he felt discomfort or worried that he might act on his jealousy in a self-destructive way.

Zachary's jealousy was so out of hand that professional help was essential. Along with psychological guidance, some of the quick fixes might assist him in his recovery.

Envy is a natural reaction when someone gets or does what

you want to get or do. When this occurs it can prompt you to get what you want for yourself. Your envy can be a positive motivator. Envy is an unproductive emotion when it does not inspire you to work for what you want, to feel no pleasure when you do achieve because you can always find someone who has done or has more, and when it drains your strength. If you are caught up in feelings that it isn't fair and hate those who have more, envy is ruining your life. If you think that good things are available in limited quantities, and if someone else appears to have many possessions, achievements, and interesting activities, you will feel shut out because you believe there won't be anything wonderful left for you. You can see that envy can be a destructive, self-defeating, insatiable emotion.

Envy was Genevieve's special problem. Although she liked her friends, she could never feel anything but depression and resentment whenever they did or received something she would have liked for herself. Unfortunately, her attitude showed. Some of her friends disliked Genevieve for her ungracious manner. Others were sensitive to her problem and tried to protect her. They stopped telling her about their achievements or acquisitions. They did not want to upset her. They did not want to deal with her reaction.

Marjorie was envious too. She wanted to own a certain model sports car. Whenever she saw one she envied the person driving it. Her envy gave her a goal. She worked until she was able to buy one for herself. She could feel happiness in her feat. She was content. She didn't look for other reasons to envy people.

Genevieve's envy was a towering problem for her. Quick fixes would give her some help, but she needs professional assistance to be able to enjoy her life and relationships without the crippling effects of her envy.

Marjorie's envy was no problem to her. If it should ever get in her way, she could profit posthaste from a few quick fixes.

• QUICK FIXES FOR •
• JEALOUSY AND ENVY •

Although jealousy and envy are different a quick fix that works for one may work for the other. Also, you do not need the task

163

of deciding what is envy and what is jealousy. Consequently, quick fixes that work for one or both are provided in this section.

───239 · Embrace Reality

Much of jealousy and envy is based on unrealistic thinking. Clarifying your thoughts to encompass reality will give you instant relief and a healthier perspective. Rearrange your ideas to coincide with the following facts.

1. No one else can bring you happiness. Although you may be happier around certain people, your happiness does not depend on their presence.

2. What another person does or does not do will not ensure your happiness. People do not do things against you as much as they do things for themselves. If they show interest in someone else or have something you have always craved, they are not doing anything to harm you. How you take what they do or have is what makes the difference.

3. Everybody can and does love more than one person. If the one you love also loves her or his parents, friends, and children it does not diminish the love he or she has for you. Love can be different for different people.

4. You cannot always be number one. Even though someone may love you completely you will never get all the attention all of the time. Intervening factors such as work responsibilities, health priorities, project intensities, and the needs of others will take time and concentration away from you. This does not mean you are loved less. It only means that energies are needed elsewhere.

5. There is enough to go around. Love is boundless. There is enough love in the world for you. If someone else gets the love you crave it is not part of a design to deprive you. It is the same with objects and honors. Everybody else can get theirs and you can have yours too.

6. Nobody does everything well. Because someone else is eloquent in his or her speech does not mean that you are less because you are not. You are good in other areas.

Remind yourself of all of these facts regularly. This will help you overcome your jealousy and envy because it will give you a healthier outlook.

——240 · Seeds of Jealousy and Envy

When, where, what, and how are the questions you must ask yourself.

When

How far back does your jealousy go? Were you first jealous of your sibling(s)? Did you notice jealousy of your classmates? Did your jealousy begin after you started dating? Did you get your toxic jealousy only after you married or after you had children?

Ask yourself the same questions regarding envy. Were you envious of what your sisters or brothers had? Did you resent your classmates' success? Have you been or are you uncomfortable with your friends' happiness? Do you find yourself feeling most envious at work? Or do you have problems when you see others with material possessions you wish were yours?

Where

Where are you when you are most jealous? Do you suffer most at parties, when your spouse is away from you, or when he or she gives someone else special attention?

Where does your envy exhibit itself? Do you find yourself unable to enjoy a stroll through a department store because you feel resentful that you cannot have everything you want? Do you have to stay away from people who apparently have more than you do?

What

What makes you jealous? Is it how your favorite person dresses or who that person is with? Are you jealous if that person makes independent decisions without first consulting you?

Is your envy global, or do certain things make you more envious than others. Is academic superiority the item that turns you green with envy? Does the skill others have in sports distress you? Do you go bananas if you see someone in an expensive car? What do you envy? Better yet, what don't you envy? Are you relaxed and content in certain areas? Try to adopt that relaxed attitude in areas in which your desire brings you agony and makes you mean-spirited.

How

How do you act when you are jealous? How do you demonstrate this feeling to those around you? Does everyone know you are jealous? Is the emotion hidden from all but those of whom you are jealous? Do you recognize your jealousy, or do you try to hide the feeling from yourself as well?

What is your behavior when you are jealous? Do you get angry, or insulting, or do you withdraw? Do you cry or pout? Do you refuse to talk about it or do you belabor it?

Ask yourself the same questions if you are envious. Do you try to make the other person's success seem small or insignificant? Do you avoid, compete with, gossip about, attempt to destroy, or malign the other person and what he or she did or has?

Once you understand the when, where, what, and how of your jealousy and/or envy you know what you have to work on. Your problem may be circumscribed and confined to one part of your life. This will make it easier to manage because you have many areas untouched by these negative emotions. If you can find no piece of your life free from excessive concern about what others do or have you will have to work much harder. But have hope, you have identified your problem.

Pansy knew her husband was attracted to brunettes. She was jealous when she saw him talking to a female with dark hair. This could happen any place and any time. All it took for her to feel jealous was to see a black- or brown-haired female. When this happened she would find herself watching her husband's every move and attributing disloyal intentions to him if he smiled, looked interested, or talked to the woman for more than one minute. At that point she would become boisterous to call attention to herself, make plans for them to leave from wherever they were, harangue him all the way home, and question him repeatedly about the girl. For days afterward she would harp about his supposed dalliance. Pansy's husband responded with a mixture of several approaches. He explained, reassured, denied, teased, got angry, and agreed, but nothing would quiet her jealousy.

When Pansy analyzed her pattern of jealousy she could more objectively realize that it was her problem, her reaction, and her own misery. She knew when, where, what, and how she reacted. She also knew that she was ruining a relationship that meant a lot to her because of the way she was expressing her jealous feelings.

Roger was happy for his friends when they were able to get the things they wanted. He enjoyed visiting them in their lovely homes, hearing about their fantastic vacations and their promotions at work. What he could not stand was their educational achievement and apparent intellectual ability. He felt overpowered by anyone with a higher degree than his or who had attended a more prestigious college, and when someone appeared to have a larger fund of knowledge than he thought he had.

This envy was a very real problem for Roger because he was always able to find people he perceived to be intellectually superior to him. They did not have to be people he knew. He could read a newspaper article about a great scholar or respected researcher and feel like a failure. All that he had achieved was as nothing compared to the eminence he saw in these other people. His bad feeling would color his entire day. He would lose his ability to enjoy or take pleasure in anything that happened. There was no cheering him up. Time had to pass before he could pull himself out of his despondency. In the meantime he was surly to those around him. After he figured out the when, where, what, and how of his envy he saw that he was causing his own anguish. He could plan a way to get himself out of his irrational thinking habit.

———241 · Follow Your Plan

Knowing your pattern of irrational jealousy or envy is only the first step, but it is a decisive step toward your quick fix. If you do not know what is making you act in a senseless manner you do not know where to start. To make a plan you need a procedure. The following outline will be helpful to you.

1. Make a list with two columns. In one column write down all the reasons you have for your jealous and envious feelings. In the column right next to it catalogue why your jealous and envious feelings are unreasonable and degrading.
2. Take the list that defines how ridiculous your feelings of jealousy and envy are and read it into a tape recorder. Listen to this tape three times a day for ten days.
3. Make a second list with a description of your reactions and behaviors when you are in a state of jealousy or envy. Next to each description write if what you do is helpful or unhelpful, constructive or destructive. If it is helpful or constructive keep it. If it is unhelpful or destructive decide to get rid of the reactions and behaviors. Do you have any you want to keep?
4. Absolutely do not do any of the unhelpful or destructive behaviors again. You may (and should) recognize your

168

feelings of jealousy and envy, but decide immediately that you are not going to respond in your typical way.

5. When you feel jealous or envious repeat to yourself all the reasons why you do not have to experience this negativity. You will find your reasons in the second column of the list you made in step one.

6. Reward yourself for changing your feelings and controlling your behavior.

Pansy and Roger will be used as continuing examples.

1. Pansy made the following lists of her reasons for her jealousy and why she had no reason to have those feelings.

REASONS FOR JEALOUSY
a. I know my husband likes brunettes.
b. Husband frequently talks to brunette women.
c. Husband looks at brunettes and smiles when he is talking to them.

WHY I NEED NOT BE JEALOUS
a. I am a brunette.
b. He also talks to blondes.
c. It is good manners to look at people when you talk with them.
d. He goes places with me and goes home with me.
e. He continues to be with me.
f. He has always said he wants to be with me.

2. Pansy intellectually understood the lists and knew that her jealousy was unfounded. But the facts did not immediately change her feelings. She recorded them on a tape recorder and listened to her reasons not to be jealous. She did this three times a day. She always listened to the tape just before she went to sleep. Interestingly, she started remembering some dreams in which she competed successfully with other brunettes for her husband's affection. She also began to have dreams in which no feelings of jealousy were sensed when she was in situations in which she would previously have responded in

169

a jealous way. She was elated to note that her subconscious was getting the message that she had no reason to be jealous of her beleaguered husband.

3. Pansy identified her reactions and behaviors as the following:

a. Make a spectacle of myself.

   a. Destructive as everybody knows what I am doing. Unhelpful because I make a fool of myself.

b. Berate husband.

   b. Destructive because I show I have no confidence in myself or my husband. Unhelpful because I won't believe what he says so he gives up.

4. Pansy vowed to give up the destructive and unhelpful behaviors. It was easier at this point because she had made her list of reasons for not being jealous and was listening to them on a regular basis.

5. Whenever Pansy felt tense and felt a twinge of jealousy, she repeated all the reasons she had for not being jealous.

6. Relief from jealousy and irrational behavior was all the reward Pansy needed. However, she felt very proud of herself when she was in situations in which she had previously been jealous so she decided to give herself an extra reward. Every time she did not succumb to jealousy she made an appointment at an elite beauty salon and bought herself the works. This not only was an effective reward, but it enhanced her self-esteem as the beauty treatment made her feel more attractive. When her jealousy reared up she made herself wear a blonde wig for a designated period of time.

Roger had work to do too. He was enjoying most of his life, but was troubled that he could not find pleasure in his own intellectual abilities because of his envy. After he convinced himself that envy was not a necessary part of his life he could develop a plan to curtail it. Maybe he was more prone to envy than other people, but that would not prevent him from being free from it.

1. Roger made a two-column list of the reasons for his envy and why the envy did not serve him well.

REASONS FOR MY ENVY	WHY I NEED NOT BE ENVIOUS
a. Others are smarter than I am.	a. I am smarter than some others. Only some people are smarter than I am.
b. If someone knows more than I do, it feels like I know nothing.	b. Whatever someone else knows does not take away from what I know. And I can learn more. I can learn from others.
c. A degree from a prestigious college would have made me feel better about myself.	c. Feeling good about myself should not depend on what university I attended. Hardly anyone pays any attention to where people went to school.
d. People are trying to make me look stupid.	d. People are trying to make themselves look good.
e. If I'm not smart, people won't like me.	e. People like me for other attributes than my brain.

2. Roger had his wife read the second column into a tape recorder. He listened to this in the morning and after he was in bed at night. He taped the list to his mirror and to his car visor and read it to himself out loud three times a day. This exposure to another point of view so indoctrinated him that after about two weeks he wondered how he had ever been so unhappily envious in the first place.

3. Roger hated the way he felt when he was envious and he also hated the way he acted. He made the following lists to address his behavior and reactions.

a. I stop having fun.	a. It is destructive for me to ruin my own social life. It

b. I withdraw and look disapproving.

       is unhelpful for me to spoil the occasion for myself.

b. It is destructive to let my negative and unreasonable feelings show. It makes me look immature and ungracious. It is unhelpful as it gives me a feeling that I have no control over myself.

c. I get surly.

c. Surliness in destructive because I take my feelings out on people who are not responsible for them. It is unhelpful as it makes me feel worse about myself.

d. I'm hard to be around for days afterward.

d. Carrying my envy with me for days gives others power over me that they do not want, nor should they have it. This is destructive. Feeling miserable for days does not make it better. It is unhelpful.

e. I am inconsolable.

e. It is destructive to not let someone else help me and to be unable to help myself. It is unhelpful to be caught in a morass of self-debasement.

4. Roger did not have to decide not to engage in his surly, joyless behavior. The facts decided this for him.

5. If Roger started to backslide into his form of envy, he

increased his references to his list and reminded himself that he was smart enough to manage the life-style he had and enjoyed. A little negative conditioning helped him too. He told himself that he looked like a fool when he engaged in the foolish behavior he demonstrated when he was feeling envious.

6. Roger knew the perfect reward for his success. Whenever he got through a tough time or when he managed not to show (and often not feel) envy during times he knew he would have in the past, he bought himself a reference book or signed up for a class he wanted to take. Not being able to improve himself in this desired fashion was aversive enough that he needed no other negative reinforcer when he acted on his feelings of envy.

——242 · Admit to Jealousy or Envy

Jealousy and envy are not admired emotions. Frequently you may not want to admit them to yourself. However, if you do not, they will give you more pain. If you pretend you are not jealous or envious when you are, you are lying to yourself. When you lie to yourself you are unable to handle, improve, avoid, or cure the problem because you are not admitting it. When you are jealous or envious own up to it. The pain you feel will be less severe and you will be able to deal with your jealousy or envy. These may be unwelcome emotions, but they are not uncommon. You are not alone in being jealous or envious when good sense tells you that you ought not to be. But being in good company does not make your behavior right. If you know your feelings, you can control the behavior that results from your feelings. You do not have to tell others about your jealous or envious feelings, but that is often helpful too.

——243 · Tell Others

If you judiciously confide your feelings of jealousy and envy you will find that your feelings are not peculiar. Others have them too. We may be thrilled at another's good fortune, but at the same time be envious that it did not happen that way for us. You may think it is fine that your siblings have done so well, but still be jealous of the pride your parents show in them.

Comedians get big laughs when they talk about their jealousy and envy by making fun of themselves. The reason their presentations are so funny is because they hit so close to home. You can use their technique. You can poke fun of your own green-eyed monster. Others will join you in humorous statements of dismay at the lack of generosity in their feelings.

Admitting human foibles such as misplaced jealousy and envy is an endearing trait. If you do so with good humor and some self-effacement, your confessions will be welcomed and appreciated. Those you talk with will feel relieved that they can then recount their similar feelings. You can all laugh at yourselves and your weaknesses. It will make the jealousy or envy easier to handle.

——244 · Identify with Yourself

You may be one of the many whose identity is tied up in another person. If that is the case, you are in a position to experience unreasonable jealousy. If the man or woman to whom you have given responsibility for yourself seems more interested in someone else than in you, you are likely to be jealous. If you look to this person for security, status, and approval your thoughts of yourself are inexplicably tied up with the other person. You are not an individual who can stand alone. What the other person is, you are. If your security with this person is threatened you become fearfully jealous. To overcome this type of jealousy, your only hope is to become your own person, to see value in yourself, and to know you can stand alone, no matter what the other person does. Your status depends on you and who you are. Approval is for you, not for the company you keep. Figure out who you are and know that you are fine. You can want to be with another person and be happier when you are, but you are still you. Identify the qualities that make you, you. Think about all the things you do to care for yourself. See that you can take care of yourself and are a separate entity.

—— 245 · Take Action

If you do feel jealous of your significant other because of the attention he or she is giving or getting, do not fume and fester. Take action. You will feel better for doing something acceptable that at the same time stakes your claim. You will not feel left out, ignored, and unwanted if you make the right move. Some of the things you can do are:

1. Go to the person and put your arm around him or her while the conversation is going on.
2. Take another person with you and join him or her and the person or persons with whom he or she is talking. Introductions can be made.
3. Ask the object of your affection or the person he or she is with to help you do something.
4. Take his or her hand and say, "Isn't he (or she) wonderful?"
5. Walk over and offer the person something to eat or drink.
6. Ask the person to accompany you to look at something or to answer a question.
7. Make an announcement to the entire group or arrange a group activity that requires everyone's attention.

   All of these actions are simple, keep you from sizzling in silence and solitude, and are innocuous. If you do them cheerfully and with confidence you will not look jealous.

—— 246 · Feel Your Own Power

If you feel you are the least powerful in a relationship you are more likely to be jealous. That can be remedied by saying to yourself, "We are equal. He or she is with me because he or she wants to be, not because I am subservient to him or her." Say this to yourself three times every time you feel powerless and jealous. Do not expect to believe it right away. You will believe it and believe in your own power as your attitude changes and as you notice your relationship is not adversely affected.

─────247 · Label It Correctly

Reactions to jealousy or envy can be mislabeled. You may prefer to say you are hurt, angry, frustrated, puzzled, disappointed, begruding, or miffed. But what you are saying is that you are jealous or envious. If you do not feel good about the attention someone is giving your special person or about what another person has or does, all the other labels are wrong. You are jealous or envious. If you label it wrong, you will not treat it correctly.

Valerie said she was miffed when her boyfriend went out with his friends and didn't invite her. She denied being jealous, saying that the behavior was puzzling to her because she would rather be with him than with her friends and could not understand that he did not feel the same way. She had to admit to jealousy before she could work on the problem with her boyfriend, or more specifically, with herself.

Walter felt like punching out his boss when she promoted a coworker over him, even though he knew that person was more qualified and had seniority over him. He felt the same rage when his neighbor was honored with the town's citizen of the year award. He disclaimed envy, but he was envious of anybody who got more recognition than he did, even when he knew the recognition was warranted. When Walter owned up to being envious he learned to control his seething.

─────248 · Put It in Perspective

Rejection of any kind is painful. But one rejection is not a sign that you will be rejected by everyone for everything. People ask each other out. Those asked out may be busy, may not want to do what they were invited to do, may be sick or tired, or not care for the person doing the asking. One rejection does not make you a reject. This is not a reason to feel envious of those who appear to be more socially successful. You do not know how many times they have been rejected and had to try again.

Yvonne asked Theodore to go to the ball game with her. Theodore said no, not because he didn't want to be with Yvonne but because he hated ball games. When she regrouped and asked him out to lunch he said yes. Yvonne's angst over the first rejection was wasted emotion. She had further expended her energy by being jealous when Theodore went to a concert with a friend of his. When she realized that Theodore was doing what he liked by accepting or rejecting an activity, she had the outlook she needed to put her jealousy in perspective and not see an initial no as a personal rejection.

─────249 · Do Not Look for the Hidden Meaning

If you see someone you care about with someone else, take it for granted that it is an accidental, business, or friendly meeting.

If some people you know appear to flaunt their new possessions or recent honors, see it as their own delight in what they have recently acquired and not as an attempt to make you envious or to make themselves look better than you.

Take what people do and what you see at face value. Do not try to analyze or look for hidden meanings that they are acting with a lack of loyalty or in an effort to lord it over you.

Take people's words and actions for what they say and do. Do not look for added significance. Do not let yourself seek out a secret agenda. If you find yourself doing this, write out the exact words you heard or the actions you saw. Every time you try to make something more out of it, read what you wrote. Do not let your imagination and suspicions enter in. Make no attempt to interpret the words or behaviors.

─────250 · Admit Your Mistake

Apologize. Say you are sorry. Explain. Admit that you were wrong. If you accuse unjustly when you are jealous or act ungraciously when you are envious, say you are disappointed in the way you acted, that your doubts were unfounded, and that you will guard against such reactions in the future. Mean what you say.

—251 · Praise Others

Practice praising others for the very things you envy. Practice enough and you will begin to believe that you are happy for another person. You will get good feedback when you tell people you are proud of them, that you admire them, and that you are delighted that all is well for them. Admire them. Don't envy them. Be glad that the world has talented people. Have gratitude for what they add to your life and the lives of others. Think of emulating them, not competing with them. Or just be thrilled that they can do what they do so well and know that you do not have to do what they do. You have your own interests.

—252 · Remember the Good Times

When you are feeling jealous, quickly remind yourself of the good things your beloved did for you. Remember the love you felt.

When you are envious think back to your accomplishments and the nice events in your life.

When you are jealous or envious, you think only of what you do not have now. If necessary, make a list of what the person you are jealous of has done for you. Record all the wonderful things in your life so you do not get swept away in your envy.

—253 · Be Satisfied

People who are envious are not satisfied with what they have. Since they are not satisfied they are envious of what everyone else has and they never find gratification in what they have. They may be healthy, rich, powerful, loved, respected, and beautiful but they are never content with their lives. If this sounds like you, work at being satisfied with what you have so you can have joy when you have more. You can develop a satisfaction with what you have by noticing that you are surrounded by nice things and nice people. Anything additional that comes your way is a bonus. You don't need it, but you are glad to get it.

254 · No Projecting

One of the reasons you are jealous of your mate may be because you do not trust yourself. You, like everyone else, are capable of projecting feelings and wishes onto another person and then being suspicious of that person, when in actuality it is yourself that you do not trust. You may have a secret desire to have an affair. You may wish you received more admiring attention. You think you might take advantage of a likely opportunity to be unfaithful. Your anxiety about your hidden wishes may be what makes you jealous of your husband, wife, girlfriend, or boyfriend. If you suspect this is the case you must continually remind yourself that the person you distrust is you. Even though you might feel disloyal or sometimes have perfidious thoughts, you have no right to project these ideas onto the person you doubt. Take care of your own feelings. Do not deny them. Do not try to accuse someone else of them. Remind yourself that it is you, not your partner, you must control.

255 · Look at What Else Is Going On in Your Life

You have stresses in your life. Sometimes you have more stress than you feel you can handle. There may be many demands on your time. You may be overworked. You may feel guilty about not having enough time to give to the people who are important to you. Since you are not able to be available and provide attention to those you care about you may feel they resent you. And they may be unhappy that you do not have time for them. This combination of facts and feelings can make you feel more dubious about your special person's activities and behaviors. Where you might not notice otherwise, you may now take note when he or she spends time with friends or engages in hobbies or stays away late at night. You get jealous. You know you are being neglectful and worry that your friend is finding someone else to do what you are not doing. Do something about your schedule. That will take care of your jealousy.

——256 · Ask for Changes

Your jealousy is your problem. However, the person on whom you focus your jealousy may inadvertently be doing something that stirs up your feelings. If this is the case, do not hesitate to make a reasonable request that the behavior be changed.

George was not consumed by jealousy, but he always acted out when he and Mabel were with her sister and brother-in-law. Mabel was disgusted with George's behavior as he was argumentative and sarcastic around the brother-in-law. The occasion regularly ended in bad feelings. Mabel did not know what to do. She wanted them all to be friends, but she could not control George's behavior. It seemed to George that Mabel was attracted to her brother-in-law, that she sided with him in discussions, and that she went along with the brother-in-law's criticism of George. George said he would be better able to manage the situation if Mabel would not appear to prefer her brother-in-law to him. Mabel had been unaware of how her behavior made George feel and she felt she could change without compromising herself and without causing problems with her relatives. In the future, Mabel did not enter in when George was being teased. In fact, she would touch George to let him know she was on his side. She did not flirt with her brother-in-law, but maintained a friendly, matter-of-fact demeanor. George was so pleased that Mabel was willing to make the effort that he felt better about her and about himself. It did wonders for their relationship and allowed their friendship with Mabel's sister and her family to flourish.

——257 · Do Not Spy, But Get the Facts

Spying is demeaning to you and to the relationship. It is often a useless expenditure of energy and emotion. It drives you, and the person you are spying on, crazy. Spying is a symptom of unreasonable jealousy and a need to control. People who are controlling push the redial button on the telephone or the beeper, interview friends and family for more information, check to see where the person is by calling or driving by; and monitor spending, mileage, and what clothes are worn. It is smothering. It does not work. You will not find out anything you probably would not have found out anyway. You will disgust the person you do not trust. You will run him or her out of your life.

But it is fine to get the facts. You may ask why your wife is especially helpful to the man who took her job after she left the company. You have a right to know why your husband was two hours late coming home from work. You are naturally curious when somebody changes his or her habits, routine, or style of dress. Noticing change and finding out the reasons for the unusual are understandable. Supervising a person's every move is not.

——258 · No Tit for Tat

If you are jealous of someone, it does not cure the problem if you decide to make him or her jealous in return.

If you are envious of your neighbor's lawn, it may make you feel better if you fix your lawn not only to match hers, but to exceed it in beauty. However, if your purpose is to help your envy by making another envious of you, you are doing nothing to fix your envy problem.

Glenda felt secure in her relationship with her father until he remarried. She then felt jealous of the new stepmother's connection with her father and was also upset that her father now had a son, albeit a stepson. She handled this threat to her status quo by trying to make her stepmother and stepbrother jealous of her. She called her father three times a day, had him come over to her house to perform handyman jobs, fixed food for him she knew he liked, took him with her to events they had always enjoyed together, and monopolized his time and attention in every way he could. She made a noble effort, but it did not make her feel better because her father still gave time and attention to the new relatives. Additionally, they were not jealous of her. They were annoyed with her. Trying to heal her own jealousy by making those she was jealous of, jealous of her,

181

did not help Glenda. It did not make her feel better and it did not work out the way she wanted it to.

Wesley was happy in his job until a new administrator took over. This person elevated one of Wesley's coworkers over him. Wesley was envious that he had not been considered for the job. He decided that he would get an administrative position and show them. They would be envious of him. He did this, but found he did not like the job. Administrative work was tedious and boring for him. And the people he wanted to envy him did not know they were supposed to and didn't.

The quick fix here is to do nothing that smacks of getting even. Take care of your jealousy or envy. Do not try to retaliate by giving people a dose of their own medicine.

———259 · Curb Your Imagination

Imagined unfaithfulness can make you as jealous as the actual act of infidelity. You can help your jealousy by curbing your imagination. Jealous people not only imagine disloyalty, seeing signs in innocent comportment, but they frequently visualize the suspected offender in compromising situations. Vivid imaginations and erroneous conclusions are extremely potent when they are combined with mind pictures. This can be combatted by changing the vision. Conjure up images of your loved one buying you gifts, sitting and thinking about you, embracing you, telling someone of your many attributes, or rushing to be with you. Whenever your brain flashes the unwanted fancies, replace them with the scenes you have prepared that show your lover reacting positively and being devoted to you. If you are going to use your imagination, use it constructively to make yourself feel better.

———260 · Do Not Ask for the Details

If you have a reason to be jealous, if there has been a dalliance, do not ask for the details. Don't make yourself feel worse. The more you know, the more you have to remember, and the more you suffer. Generally speaking, what you imagine is often worse than the facts. However, if the situation involves jealousy that is not the case. If you suspect it, you still do not know. If you know, your fears are confirmed. If you know, you will find constant reminders of the past. If you know, you will bring up the transgression in moments of anger. The less you know, the better off you will be. The only important thing for you to know is that whatever happened is in the past and there is no intention of repeating it. Never utter, "If I knew the truth, I would feel better." Bite your tongue. All you need to know is that it is over.

——261 · Co-opt Them

Are you jealous or envious of a person or persons? This will not do when you can do something about it. Do you want what they

have? Get to be their friend. Be part of what they do. Be included. Make them part of your ventures. Have them on your side. Nancy Friday writes in her book *Jealousy* that she was not aware of her envy of the beautiful girls she grew up with because she not only became their best friend, she became their leader.[1]

———262 · Do Not Expect Anything

There is a philosophy that if you do not expect anything, you will not be disappointed and you will be pleasantly surprised when you get something.

Not expecting anything can help you with envy. If you do not expect anything you will not be spent with envy when your mother leaves your sister her jewelry, when your coworker gets recognition for a project you helped write, or when your friend wins the all-expense vacation trip. You can be relaxed about these events while you still enjoy the good things that happen to you. If you can get it into your head that no one owes you anything, that you can provide for yourself, but that good luck occurs occasionally, you will be able to manage your tension when others get what you would have liked. You can get a real thrill out of whatever you do get. This will save you from sibling brawls over who gets what after the death of a relative, and from petty comparisons about who does what for whom. It will also save you from anxiety over gift giving and receiving, and worry about getting what you feel is due you in work, friendship, and family situations.

When Ivan's father died he left his money to be divided between his two children in equal parts. However, he bequeathed his house to his son, Harris, who had cared for him in this home for two years before he died. The father did not specify how his furniture and other possessions should be distributed. Harris took responsibility for them, giving Ivan his father's stamp collection and some clothes. He kept everything else for himself and stayed in the house. Ivan wanted and expected more. He felt that his father favored Harris because Harris was closer to his father. He even accused Harris of influencing their father when he was weakened by illness. Harris was astonished by Ivan's reaction. He thought he was carrying out his father's wishes and that he had earned the house and possessions because of the care he had given his father. Ivan felt nothing buy envy and animosity. Ivan had always been jealous of Harris, who seemed to be able to please his father, whereas he had not. This situation exacerbated the jealousy. Because of Ivan's envy and long-standing jealousy the sibling relationship was further strained. If Ivan had not expected certain material remembrances from his father, he would not have ended up with his feelings of rejection and anger. He could have enjoyed what he did get and kept a more positive relationship with his brother.

For further help for envy and jealousy, see Chapter 5 Lack of Self-Confidence.

• NOTES •

1. Nancy Friday, *Jealousy* (New York: William Morrow and Company, Inc., 1985).

Chapter SEVEN

ANGER

SINCE THIS BOOK is devoted to quick fixes for your personal problems, this chapter's focus is on handling your own, not other people's anger. However, if you can manage your own anger you will be better able to cope with the anger of others. The more uncomfortable you are with your own fury, the more helpless you will feel around others who are expressing their anger.

Anger has acquired a bad reputation. In fact, anger is a normal, constructive emotion that is part of the mortal makeup for good reason. Anger is there so you can use it in situations in which normal anger is appropriate. The key phase here is, you can use it. Anger, like other feelings, is an attribute of your humanness. Anger, like other emotions, is a feature to benefit people. If you are denying your anger, you are not using it to your advantage. If you cannot control your anger, you are a hazard to yourself and to others. Feelings are part of you and are there to serve you, not to rule you.

Anger is part of you, whether or not you admit it. Dangerous as it is, people can and have learned to deny their anger. They have become so good at it that they no longer acknowledge that they have it. Anger repression, a putting away of the emotion, becomes automatic. If you find yourself saying that you never get angry, you have trained yourself to banish your angry thoughts and feelings without consciously knowing that you are doing it. Although there may be some comfort in being free of the physical and mental reaction to rage, disallowing your true feeling of anger does not solve the problem as you still have anger. You are hiding it from yourself and are dealing

187

with it in a destructive way. Pushing anger away is not in your best interest because it appears in other ways. You may not look angry, but you may be a backbiter, or be persistently late for appointments. You may develop migraines, ulcers, colitis, arthritis, high blood pressure, asthma, or just not feel well. You may find flaws, become pointedly silent, forget important dates or items, or be sarcastic and devoid of all feelings. You may become a complainer, depressed, bored, a nitpicker, a nag, an alcoholic or overeater, a malicious gossiper, a whiner, a blamer, a cynic, or physically tense. In other words, your anger comes out in decidedly unattractive ways, hurts you, and deprives you of its usefulness.

When Patrick was young he had a temper. When he got angry he started throwing punches. Since he was small he often came out a loser in these altercations. Sometime around his twelfth birthday and shortly after he had lost a tooth to an opponent who responded violently to being hit, Patrick decided he was not going to get angry anymore. He did not discuss his problem with anyone, so he did not explore alternative ways for managing his anger. He just knew he didn't want to get hurt any more and his angry feelings were causing him pain, so his logical conclusion was to stop his anger. This he did. It took work, but he succeeded. He became admired for his stoicism and his unhurried, calm, unruffled manner. His girlfriend, expressive and excitable, was drawn to his placid ways. They made her feel safe. They married and lived miserably ever after. Victoria, Patrick's wife, found that he was all that he was advertised to be. He was quiet. He was emotionless. He was also dull and unresponsive. If she wanted to talk to him about a problem, he got a headache. If she was upset he left the house. If she sought a confrontation he would agree with anything and then do as he pleased. If she pushed, he withdrew. Since she wanted reactions she kept pushing, and he kept withdrawing. Since he could not show anger, he found he could not show other emotions either. Victoria did not know if she was loved and cherished. She felt like an unattached satellite circling out of reach. When she threatened to leave him he agreed to a last-ditch effort. They went to marriage counseling. During this process he showed that he had more fear of his anger than he had of losing his marriage. The marriage collapsed because Victoria decided she could not live in a passionless relationship.

Gertrude, like Patrick, had a temper. She warned people that they should not make her angry as she had no control over her temper and did not know what she might do. When she got angry she reacted immediately and without thought. She would feel the wrath build up and she would start yelling. She was insulting, foulmouthed, and threatening. She vowed vengeance and could not let go of her anger until she did some sort of harm to the person who had angered her. Her life was taken up with her anger. Since she was convinced that her anger controlled her, rather than vice versa, she was always busy getting angry and then getting even. Since she was caught in this negative cycle she found little time for constructive action and pleasurable pursuits on her own behalf. She spent her life alienated from most people, with few enjoyable moments, and with feelings that the world was against her.

Although Gertrude's anger was overt, and out there for the world to see, it did not serve her any better than Patrick's anger served him. She was a firm believer in acting on her anger. It is true that anger must be handled. Unfortunately, her action was without thought and there was no effort to handle it. She became her anger, instead of making her anger part of her repertoire of feelings.

Gertrude's temper was violent, but confined to verbal assaults and plans of revenge. Grady, however, was physically violent when he was angry. In his family punishment was physical. When he misbehaved he received a beating. The men in his family were given to brawling and to fighting for what they wanted. He continued the tradition. The adrenalin engendered by his anger had him on his feet and striking out without thought whenever he felt provoked. He hit and he threw things; the walls of his house were full of holes. His wife and children knew to get out of his way when he was riled. He was frequently picked up for public fighting and was jailed when he hit a police officer when he was stopped for a traffic ticket. This made him more angry. He felt justified in his anger as he felt he was treated unfairly. His downward spiral was predictable. He could not hold a job because he fought with his coworkers and rebelled against authority. His family left him out of terror. His trouble with the law continued. It took the justice system to get Grady the help he needed.

What is this powerful emotion, anger? Does it have a purpose? Is there good and bad anger?

Anger is as common as hunger, as normal as breathing, and is part of the standard equipment that comes with each human being. Anger is neither right, nor wrong. It is how anger is handled that is either right or wrong. Anger has a purpose. It is a way to communicate how you feel. It is good to show appropriate feeling when you are expressing anger. You can look and sound angry when you are. This gives a clear, unambiguous message. Angry feelings are yours to use when you admit to them. Then you can express your anger in constructive and fitting ways.

As you read this you may think of many reasons why anger is not a good emotion to have. You may remind yourself of all the ways anger can get you into trouble. There are many ways. But there are also ways to govern your anger to avoid the trouble that mismanaged anger can bring you. Quick fixes for anger will help you do that. However, be aware that you live in a culture that does not value anger and praises people who give no evidence of anger by saying:

Not a mean bone in their bodies.

They never had a bad word to say about anybody or anything.

They would never hurt a fly.

They can take it.

They never lose it.

They are gentle as lambs.

They will do anything for you.

You can take them anywhere.

They don't make waves.

You may also notice that anger and rage are emotions that are often denied by how they are labeled. The angry feeling may be downgraded by calling it frustration, irritation, resentment, bitterness, hurt, tension, or disappointment. This sugarcoating somehow makes it more acceptable. It may be low-voltage anger. But it is anger. Accept the fact that you too get angry. Be proud of your full set of human emotions. Recognize what makes you angry. Do any of the following bring out your hostility?

People putting you down.

Sarcasm.

Losing a game.

People wanting more than you are willing to give.

Being laughed at.

Not being taken seriously.

Being ignored.

Feeling helpless.

Not getting what you want.

Hearing phrases such as: If I were you, everybody else does it, how dare you, why do you, where have you been, do you always do that.

Feeling threatened

Feeling disapproval.

Not getting your way.

Someone taking credit for your work.

Getting blamed unfairly.

Knowing you are not doing your best.

Feeling inferior or unimportant.

Not getting any privacy.

Being rejected.

Being criticized.

Being accused.

People talking behind your back.

Traffic problems.

Irritating habits of others.

People expecting you to wait on them.

People not showing consideration of you.

People not listening.

People dismissing your feelings.

Indecisiveness.

People who only talk about themselves.

Gum chewing.

Smoking.

People goofing off.

People using things and not putting them back in the right place.

Company that stays too long.

You are perfectly normal if you picked most or all of the items in this list as anger makers. There are many everyday things to get angry about. You may want to review the chapter on stress to determine ways to handle the irritations of day-to-day living.

Don't cop out on your anger. Don't say I have no control, the feelings take over, or I am no longer responsible when I get angry, or I don't get angry, or anger is a useless emotion. Be aware that out of control anger and denied anger are as unhealthy as acknowledged and expressed anger is useful and physically and emotionally healthy.

Your body has a normal physiological response to anger. This is not unhealthy. Anger that is chronic or suppressed is harmful. Anger that is managed is not destructive.

When you are angry your body experiences a biochemical change. Adrenalin is secreted in greater than normal amounts. More blood is circulated. The heart speeds up. The cholesterol level rises. Blood pressure goes up. The pupils dilate. The intestines shut down. Breathing is short and rapid. You are tense, apprehensive, and ready. This is all fine, unless you stew or explode. Poor anger management results in cancer, heart failure, accident, and suicide rates that are 50 percent higher in chronically angry people than for those with less hostility.

Now that you are convinced that anger is normal and that you can take control of it, it is time to introduce you to some quick fixes for anger.

• QUICK FIXES FOR ANGER •

——263 • Acknowledge Anger

The first step in anger rehabilitation is to acknowledge that you have anger. This will help you if you hide your anger or express it without restraint. But there are two different problems here. The denier will have to relearn to recognize normal anger. The exploder will have to pause and take the extra step that encourages thoughtful action instead of an unharnessed re-action.

The anger stuffer needs reeducation. This can be self-education, but it is very helpful to have a coach. Since you have learned to ignore your feelings of anger it is automatic for you not to recognize instances in which normal anger is the right response. Whether or not you have someone to help you, some independent work is necessary. The following instructions will assist you in reclaiming your emotional life.

1. Make a list of incidents that you think might cause you or someone else to feel anger. This list might include insults, put-downs, threats, scams, lies, and violence. Beside each general category, write out a specific example, preferably from your own life. If you cannot conjure up anything personal use something that happened to someone you know. If that too escapes you, take something from the newspaper or television.

2. Read the newspaper and watch television. Make a note of each incident of anger you read about or observe. Notice how people handled their anger.

3. Take an interest in other people's actions and reactions. Carry a notepad with you and write out each instance of observed anger. Begin to notice how others manage their anger. Try to increase your skill in recognizing anger by paying attention to incidents that look as though they would bring about a normal anger reaction.

4. Each evening, make a review of your day. Try to pick out occurrences that might have provoked normal anger if you had been tuned in to that emotion.

This is good work for you to do on your own. There will not be a scarcity of examples as anger is all around you. As you continue this exercise, you will be desensitizing yourself to the feared emotion. You will learn that anger is normal and healthy. How you handle anger is what determines whether or not it serves you well or is your enemy.

If you have access to an anger coach, you have an edge because this person can help you recognize normal anger. Ask your coach to point out situations that would bring about normal anger as they occur and are observed. This could be an incident that happens to you or to someone else. Since it is unlikely that your coach is with you all the time, tell your coach about your day. As you go over your day your coach can pull out the examples in which anyone else might well have felt infuriated. Also, have your coach alert you to his or her anger. Discuss the feelings and reactions of your coach. Observe that anger has not destroyed him or her, that it is a useful emotion, and that recognition of anger does not make you an angry person.

If you are an anger reactor, you can follow a similar procedure to help you recognize your anger prior to reacting to it. Your independent work is as follows.

1. Make a list of the events that cause you to act out. Next to the incidents write your reactions. Then list the results of your anger reactions.

2. Make a note of each newspaper report of circumstances that occurred because of action caused by anger. Watch television and take notes on displays or reports about anger. Always pay close attention to how the anger is handled and resolved. Are the results to the advantage or the disadvantage of the person or persons expressing anger? How could the anger have been handled to make it better?

3. Be alert as you go about your daily life. What happens to people when they get angry? How do they act? Do their responses serve them well or hurt them? Keep an ongoing list of as many different ways to handle anger as you can find.

4. At the end of each day make a review. When were you angry and how did you handle your anger?

This individual work is important to you as you are taking stock of your own anger. If you can tolerate help from someone without getting too angry at her or him ask her or him to be your anger coach. If this is a person who is frequently by your side, work out a signal so he or she can alert you to an adverse anger reaction. Train yourself to respond to this physical or verbal sign. It could be a hand signal, a look, or a word. Tune into it and take stock of your feelings and reactions, and re-group to evaluate and discuss what you are doing. Always remind yourself that you are trying to help yourself, that your coach is following your directions, and that you appreciate what your coach is doing on your behalf.

When your coach is not available to you and you find yourself in a situation that causes you anger, try to remember as much about it as you can and go over it with your coach at a later time. Read the rest of this chapter so you can come up with your own alternative ways for managing your anger. You will feel better about yourself if you can suggest better responses on your own. Even though you requested the help, it is not always easy to take advice.

264 • Talk Yourself Out of It

Talking yourself out of your anger is much different than ignoring your anger. Ignoring your anger is a bad practice because it leads to stuffing it, not acknowledging it, and cutting yourself off from your emotional life. When you take the first important step of knowing you are angry, you can use the quick fix of talking yourself out of it. Always remember that anger is normal and available to you. It is your choice. At times your anger may be inappropriate. At times your anger may be dangerous. At times you may decide it isn't worth it.

You want to feel your anger. Talking yourself out of it occurs after you feel the surge of indignation in your system. You do not want to stop this. You want to take control of what you do after you have this feeling.

Talking yourself out of your anger does not imply that your anger is wrong or illegitimate. You may be totally in the right to feel angry. Talking yourself out of your anger suggests that you choose not to act on your anger in this instance and that it is not worth your time and trouble.

Refer to the list of irritating events in the introduction to this chapter. Many of these anger makers are not worth the energy that anger takes. Traffic is a prime example of this. If others sharing the road with you are rude, poor drivers, out of sync with the traffic flow, or in your way, you are wasting your anger if you let their inept driving rile you. In fact, your anger may make an irritating situation a hazardous one if you act on it and take unneces-

195

sary and frightening risks. Anger in traffic is dangerous, inappropriate, and not worth it. If you spend part of each day in traffic, you particularly want to talk yourself out of uncontrolled habitual anger in such a situation as you are only hurting yourself when you persist in your angry feelings at such times. The next time a car cuts you off, feel your anger but take conscious control of it by talking yourself out of it. Recognize that the other driver is a jerk. Tell yourself that he or she failed driver's education and does not know any better. Think that maybe the driver has an emergency and is acting out of desperation. Give yourself credit for driving defensively and avoiding an accident. Refuse to let the other driver's actions ruin your day. Identify his or her actions as impersonal. Know that the driver is not driving that way to cause you harm or to upset you. Laugh at the driver's imbecility. Know that what he or she does is probably not going to hinder your progress or accelerate hers or his.

By talking yourself out of this anger you will keep yourself from chronic, ineffective anger reactions, feel more in control, and be in a better mood for the entire day. You will be an inspiration for everyone.

Peter was in a rage every time his neighbors left the garbage cans in front of their house all day. Since they did this regularly he was furious two days a week. Soon he found he was upset anticipating the twice-weekly event. Luckily he figured out that he was destroying himself with his reaction and decided that he had to manage his anger. He told himself that his neighbors were not leaving their garbage cans at the curb to aggravate him. He knew mornings were a busy time for them and every minute counted. Sometimes the refuse workers arrived after the neighbors left for the day. He noticed that other people probably had the same problem as other cans were left out all day on garbage collection day. He acknowledged that they gathered up the cans as soon as they arrived home. He still did not like it. But he did not let the garbage cans ruin his day.

——265 · Sayings That Help

Talking yourself out of anger works, but you may need a trigger to give you the pause that allows you to get to the point at which you can talk yourself out of it. To keep yourself from rage without thought, let the first indication of anger prompt you in the direction of reflection instead of reaction. Some sayings that may work for you are

I am not going to let this get to me.
Words can't hurt me.
I can be above this.
This is not right or wrong, just a difference of opinion.
This isn't worth it.
Don't get bent out of shape.
I'm taking myself too seriously.
Easy does it.
Let it go.
This is not important.
I don't need to prove myself to them.
They can't get to me.
This doesn't concern me.
I'd rather live to fight another day.
Getting upset won't help.
I can cope with this.

——266 • Don't Put People on the Defensive

One way to avoid rage-inducing situations is to make sure others are not put on the defensive. Certain unpleasant questions sound offensive and make people defensive. This means that they feel attacked and will strike back. In return, you may get angry and the scene will get ugly. Do not put yourself in that position.

Avoid confrontational questions that make you sound like an interrogator or an accuser. Do not bait people with questions that cannot possibly be answered, such as, "So you read a lot, tell me how your reading could benefit me," or "What is your plan for saving the world?"

Don't ask why. That is like asking someone to justify his or her actions. It sounds threatening to the recipient of the question. In the first place he or she may not know why. In the second place she or he may not want to tell you why. Do not ask, "Why did you do that?" or "Why do you go to work the same way every day?"

Personal questions are not only bad manners, but they can

be very intrusive. Don't ask people what they weigh, what size they wear, how old they are, or what they paid for an item. They may be polite, but they will be offended. And they will get back at you for it, if they can, unless they know some quick fixes for anger and realize you aren't worth the effort of retaliation because no one with savvy would ask such questions.

Avoid leading questions or questions that try to force agreement. Examples of these are, "Don't you agree that you waste money on your hobby?" "Aren't you in agreement with the reorganization plan?" and "You do think I'm right, don't you?" Ask instead for people's opinions, feelings, and suggestions. Give options. Keep your questions open-ended.

You may be faced with similar uncomfortable questions and feel defensive and get angry. How can you keep yourself in control, manage to duck the questions, and not get defensive? How about saying, "I don't want to talk about it?" If the questioner persists you can counter with delaying tactics by saying, "Later," "Not now," or "I'll get back to you." Or you can repeat, "I don't want to talk about it."

Or you can do as politicians do. You can talk about something else. If you are asked a question that makes you simmer you can change the subject or discourse on a related topic. So if someone says, "Don't you think it is ridiculous for you to mow your lawn every week?" you can say, "My neighbor's have been on vacation and have no one to take care of their lawn. They went to Oregon. I got a card from them last week and they are having a wonderful time. They don't know when they will be back." You can go on like this indefinitely or turn the question back to the inquisitor by asking if he or she has a recommendation or if he or she knows of someone who will take care of lawns, or at some point ask him or her about favorite vacations.

Another technique is to make exceptions for people who appear socially inept. This is in contrast to taking exception to what they say or do. Instead of getting defensive, tell yourself that they are trying to be sociable and do not know how. Understand that they may be trying to look intelligent or important, but are looking belligerent instead. Take pity on them as people. But you still don't have to answer their questions. You can hate the question and deflect it. You can evade the questioner, but don't waste your enmity on him or her.

Laugh. The question may be so outrageous and so provoking that it is preposterous. Laughing in someone's face may be uncivil and as maddening as the original question, but a smile and a saying may work very well. If they ask, "How can you still be in favor of _____?" you can grin and say that old habits die hard, or that you are a creature of habit or come up with some other cliché such as that you are stuck in your ways. How about, "She needs all the friends she can get," or "I'm loyal to a fault."

——267 · Explosions Do Not Help

Research has revealed that acting out violently does not dissipate your anger. In fact, forcible physical and verbal expressions of rage intensify anger. Know you are angry and then know what you are going to do with your anger. Do not explode without thought. This will decrease your ability to be the master of your anger and may cause you to get into trouble with people or may cause problems with the law. You may hurt someone, even yourself, and you may destroy your possessions or the belongings of others. You want to learn to control your explosive, uncontrolled anger. If you start to yell, stop yourself as soon as you possibly can. If you feel overwhelmed by your anger, get away from the situation as fast as you can.[1] Give yourself permission to think instead of lashing out. Although you may not know what to do with your anger, you have achieved a quick fix if you contain your anger. You know you are angry. You have controlled your anger. Now you can decide what to do with your anger. Read on.

——268 · State Your Anger

Be assertive, not aggressive. "I am angry," is a perfectly correct statement. You can say, "I get angry when I am treated like a dummy." You are not accusing. You are not threatening. You are stating your feeling and explaining why you feel the way you do. You can go further and say," I don't want to be treated

199

that way." Now you have described your emotional state, explained why you feel that way, and asked for what you want. Even if you do not get what you want, you have handled your anger constructively. You can be assured of a better response to a rational request than to an angry demand.

Travis was in a funk because he could not figure out how to raise the money to buy the house his growing family needed. When, in a fit of frustration, his wife accused him of being responsible for their crowded condition, Travis felt a surge of anger. He was ready to scorch the air with slurs about his wife's lack of support and poor money management, and to include threats to leave her and the children to struggle alone. Instead he took a quick time-out, composed himself so he could speak without yelling, and said, "That makes me very angry. When I am trying to right the problem every way I know how I am hurt and furious that you accuse me of doing nothing and being totally responsible for our difficulties. Instead, I would like us to write out a plan for getting what we want and discuss joint efforts for achieving our plan."

Travis's approach calmed the tense time and led to a meeting of minds and a cooperative effort. Their children were able to come out of the rooms they had fled to when they saw the fight coming on.

——269 · Count to Ten

This old saw still works. If you count to ten or twenty or one hundred, you give yourself a breather. You can collect yourself. You can step back before you do something you may be sorry for later.

——270 · Deplore Bitterness

When you are bitter you give the person you are angry with more power over you than they want or deserve. Your bitterness keeps your anger alive long after the object of your anger has forgotten about the whole thing. If you are going to stay bitter, remember that you are doing this to yourself. No one is making you react this way.

Carrying a grudge is the same thing as remaining bitter.

You are eaten away and are not hurting the person with whom you are angry. You do not want to hurt yourself so let go of your bitterness and your grudges. If you can see that it is in your best interest to let go, you can see that bitterness and grudges do you no good.

Even worse, bitterness and grudge carrying contribute to a sludge in your system. If you haven't cleared yourself of old angers, the new angers are fueled by them. Your grudges and your bitterness keep you an angry, easily ignited bomb that will go off without warning, and cause you to overreact in situations that may not call for any reaction.

You may wonder how to get rid of your bitterness and your grudges. Resolve to do it. Use your intellect to take control of your feelings of anger. Review some of the sayings that help. Decide that you do not want to do this to yourself. Realize that it is possible to let go. You are the one holding onto your anger. You can be the one to let go of it.

——271 · Do Not Displace Anger

If you do not recognize your anger and take care of it as it happens, there are other dangers besides bitterness and carrying a grudge. You may end up taking your anger out on an innocent person. This is called displaced anger. You are upset with your boss and you scream at your children. Traffic gets to you and you kick the dog. Your spouse has been nagging you and you snarl at your coworker. So your anger ends up causing you more unpleasantness and difficulty because you spread it around and make other people feel hurt and puzzled. What did they do to deserve such treatment? Now you have more reasons to be angry because you have more people angry at you. Know when you are angry and know where to direct your anger. Don't go around gathering up more anger. Passing along your anger will not help you get over it or feel better.

——272 · How Would You Like To Be Treated?

How would you like to be treated if someone was angry with you? Imagine the scene. It is likely that your desires reflect the desires of others who are confronted by an angry person. Try treating those with whom you are angry the way you would like to be treated. You probably would like to know that the person is angry and why he or she is angry. You would like to know what you can do about the problem. And you would like a chance to reasonably present your side.

——273 · If You Must Act on Anger

You may be given to physical activity and cannot quietly think out your anger and plan what you want and how to use the correct words to get it. If that is the case, substitute an activity

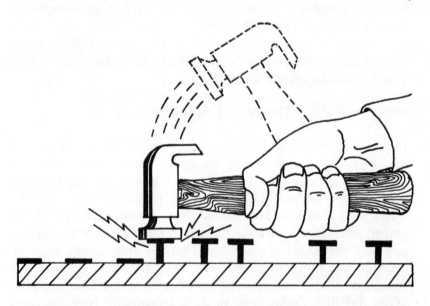

to drain off your adrenalin. Walk, pace, run. Play tennis or handball. Wash the windows or the car. Mop the floor. Brush the dog. Pound nails. Do whatever you choose until your anger is within your control.

——274 · Keep an Anger Diary

Keeping a daily anger diary will help you get in touch with your feelings and assist you in handling explosive anger. Each day write down your feelings, what caused the feelings, how you felt about your feelings, and how you reacted to the feelings. If you have friends and family you trust and can talk with, discuss these instances with one or more of them. Make plans for taking care of your anger. Get their feedback and revise your plans if their suggestions make sense to you. Try out your plan next time you feel anger. Write that in your diary.

Ruth kept a diary. She needed to learn about her feelings so she wrote in it every day, including happy, sad, and angry feelings. She noticed that she did not react to anger-arousing situations. She was often not aware of what happened until she settled down to write in her diary at the end of the day. She then understood why she had gone around feeling as though a black cloud was hanging over her all day. Since she knew that she was not showing her anger, much less acknowledging it, in the proper time and place, she decided to discuss the problem with her best friend. Together they devised a plan. They outlined situations Ruth was likely to encounter that would generate anger in most people. She was to say to herself that she would be within her rights to feel angry and try to get in touch with her angry feelings. This was step one for Ruth. As she kept her diary and became more aware she revised her plans with the help of her friend. Before long she felt she could be on her own as anger had become a normal, healthy emotion for her.

Virgil was easily offended. He could interpret the most innocuous statement in a derogatory way. He would excoriate the speaker with pejoratives. His target would be puzzled by Virgil's reaction, but not so puzzled that there was a loss of words. Retaliation was usually frequent and fast. Virgil wondered why he seemed to have so many more disagreeable run-ins than other people. He started to keep track of them in his daily diary. He shared his reports that delineated his feelings and reactions with his long-suffering girlfriend. He listened to her interpretation. Together they made a plan. Virgil's diary began to reflect fewer traumatic incidents and better relationships with the people he encountered. He felt more in control. Because of his increased control and more realistic interpretations he felt much better about himself and his life.

——275 · Face Your Fears About Anger

You may be hesitant to recognize your anger or show it because you fear that you will get out of control, that the emotion is stronger than you are. Or you may place a high priority on approval and acceptance by others and think that showing anger will bring on disapproval and rejection. This is untrue. You do not have to get out of control, and being supersweet is not going to make you more popular than the people who know when they are angry and know how to make their anger work for them. Banish your fears. You are working on the wrong end of the problem. Work on how to develop an appropriate and healthy anger that serves your needs. Do not concentrate on casting out your anger. You will be more successful when you use your anger than you will be in denying anger. This may be hard at first, but it gets easier and easier as you integrate healthier habits and feel emotionally more able.

Do not be afraid to get angry about little things. Holding the accumulated anger in leads to displaced or inappropriate anger. It is better to acknowledge your little irritations along the way and appropriately express the anger, or decide to say nothing (but only after you know what your feelings are), than to push your feelings aside.

And do not worry about getting angry at somebody to whom you are also grateful. It is possible to be indebted to people and still be upset with them. You can love a person and be furious simultaneously. These are not abnormal feelings of an out-of-control person. These are normal human emotions. You may decide not to make a big deal out of anger when it is associated with a person you really care about. Or you may care enough to let the individual know how you really feel. Just be sure you know how you feel. What you do with your feelings is a matter of choice.

——276 · Use Cold Courtesy

Judith Martin, known far and wide as Miss Manners, suggests using cold courtesy to express anger. She maintains that this is civilized, proper, and effective. She recommends that the following polite phrases be delivered in a shocked tone with an astonished look on your face.

I beg your pardon.

I believe you are gravely mistaken.

Perhaps you are unaware of the fact that _____.

Perhaps I did not make myself clear.

How dare you?[2]

——277 · Fantasize

When you are angry and you cannot do anything about it you can fantasize about what you would like to do. There are places in which you cannot readily show your anger. You may not want to let your boss know what you think of her in a staff meeting. You may not want to make a scene in a public place. You may not want to challenge a sick relative. But you may still be angry. You feel constrained by the person or the situation and cannot say or do as you would like. But you can think. People cannot read your mind and thinking does not require you to act. You can imagine anything you want. You can see yourself spouting invectives, maiming and torturing, challenging and winning, or intimidating. You can visualize anything you want. You can daydream until you have worked out your anger privately and in your head. Then you can do what is necessary considering the circumstances.

——278 · Make a Date for Discussion

Your schedule may be so busy that you don't have time to take care of your anger. When that happens you become a disgruntled, unhappy person to have around. Others feel as though you are angry at them, but, if you don't tell them they don't know why. If you are on the run and cannot take care of your anger or discuss what has made you angry because of time limitations, be sure to get an appointment to talk things out with the people involved. By the time you get to it, it may no longer seem important. Discuss it anyway. If you say it doesn't matter, you add it to your inner junk pile. You may also choose to set a later time and place to discuss anger when you or your companion are too angry to discuss anything. You can be angry. You can collect your thoughts. You can cool off. Then you can talk. Then you can work on solving problems. You are not retreating. You are saving the situation. You are making it possible to use your anger constructively by using the energy it creates to address your concerns and look for solutions.

——279 · See Anger as a Building Block

If no one knows what is making you angry, no one can do anything about what he or she is doing. He or she may guess, but is likely to guess wrong. Explaining what makes you angry, why you get angry about it, and what you would like changed gives you the opportunity to be honest in any relationship that is important to you, and gives both of you a chance to mend what is flawed. See anger as a tool to use to fix what is wrong with your association. Anger gives you an opening for putting your feelings into words and action.

——280 · Do Not Incite Yourself

It is repeatedly stressed that knowing your own anger is a good thing. But inflaming your own anger is self-defeating. Know why you are angry, but don't make it worse for yourself. Monitor your reactions to weed out the following type of self-talk.

"Who does he think he is to treat me like this?"
"I can't allow that kind of thing."
"Does she think she is better than I am?"
"He is trying to bait me."
"I cannot be taken for granted!"
"She is doing that to get to me."
"He is against me."
"She is trying to embarrass me."
or

"Nobody is going to walk on me."
"I'm not going to let him get away with that."

"I'll get even."
"If she tries that again I'll let her have it."

Even though you have these thoughts and think there is truth to them, do not dwell on them. Stick to the actual facts of what happened and develop a plan for dealing with the person or the situation in a way that best suits you.

281 · Justifying the Anger of Others

Everybody has enough irritations in the average day to warrant a head of steam. The store clerk was rude and uncooperative. You got left on hold on the telephone for ten minutes. The car did not start. Your new shoes got soaked in the rain. Your friend was late for lunch. You got a letter from the Internal Revenue Service. Since life is a series of frustrations and a constant maintenance problem, you could spend your life in a state of disgust if you can put your mind to it. Instead you might consider putting your mind to rising above all the mundane happenings of day-to-day life. Justify the other person's action. Say to yourself:

"The store clerk is having a rough day."

"The secretary is busy, calls are piling up, he or she is new at the job and doesn't know what is going on."

"The mechanic fixed one thing, but did not notice the other. He or she will be able to fix my car. The car needs attention anyway."

"It isn't raining just to get at me."

"My friend is always late. I should plan accordingly. Maybe he or she got held up (in traffic, by the boss, on the telephone)."

"My accountant did not do anything wrong to get me in trouble. He or she will help me with the IRS. It probably is a simple mistake that will take little effort."

282 · Humor Helps

In *Anger: The Misunderstood Emotion,* Carol Tavris states that you cannot laugh and frown at the same time. She recommends that you get out of your angry mood by watching a comedy or doing anything that will give you a good laugh. She suggests that "for the small indignities of life, the best remedy is almost always a Charlie Chaplin movie."[3]

You can take humor one step further by making a tense situation into a funny scene. See the ridiculous. Create outlandish reasons and excuses in your mind. Make it hilarious. A word of caution. Do not make fun of the person who is angry.

Leslie said, "Good morning," to her coworker, only to be greeted with a "What's good about it?" Now it was Leslie's choice. She could brood about the discourteous response. She could give a blistering retort. She could ignore what happened. She could ask the coworker if she wanted to talk about it. She could state how the response made her feel. She could laugh it off.

Leslie knew she felt a flair of anger at the snarly reaction to her pleasant greeting. She decided she did not want to make an issue out of it. She did not want it to ruin her day. She didn't have time to get into her coworker's problem and frankly, did

not want to hear about it even if she had the time. She did not want to ignore her own feelings. She decided to laugh it off. She saw herself answering the other employee with glowing reports of what was good about the day, going on and on about the perfect ozone level, the red convertible she saw on the way to work, the traffic light she missed, and her daughter's first tooth. As she imagined the person's awed look upon hearing a long speech about inane, but pleasant, events she began chuckling to herself. This tack further helped Leslie as it refocused her thoughts on the positive aspects of her day.

──283 · Defuse Anger

Studies conducted on men and women confronted with anger resulted in the finding that women are more likely to defuse the anger rather than meet anger with anger. In certain situations this is a skill that is useful. It is a skill that anyone can learn. It is a skill that may be helpful to you. You may want to mollify an angry boss, an irate friend, a fuming spouse, or an individual with whom you are not personally connected, whose anger is directed at you. Meeting anger with anger under most of these conditions will make it worse, and you may be the loser. If you know your feeling, you can then weigh the advantages and disadvantages of responding in kind. If you decide you are better off if you make an effort to conciliate, here are some techniques to use.

If your boss says, "You made a mistake and cost the company money," and her tone of voice indicates that she is furious, you want to get to the point at which rational analysis is possible. Even if you are right and the boss is wrong, do not get defensive. Do not yell back. Keep your voice quiet, your words measured. Ask, "Can you tell me more?" Suggest, "There may be some alternatives." Appeal, "Can you help me with this?" Submit, "We need to talk."

When your friend says, "You told Terry my secret that I asked you not to tell anyone," you need to be able to think on your feet. If you are guilty, don't lie. If you are not guilty, don't retaliate with a counter accusation. If you want to keep your friend, you want to work out the problem. You don't want to cause a rift because of the acrimony. Disarm him or her by agreeing. Say, "You are right." Offer to explain. Apologize. Accepting responsibility for your wrongdoing takes away much of the anger aimed at you and gets you to the point at which you can discuss or negotiate. If the charge is wrong, do not exacerbate the tension by asking threatening questions such as, "How can you believe that?" or "Who told you that lie?"

Should your spouse say, "I just can't stand how you treat me when we are around your friends," show your interest in hearing his or her concern by giving feedback to indicate that you really want to understand the problem. Paraphrase, "You don't like the way I am toward you when my friends are present?" Question further. Find out the specific objection and then work with him or her. What does he or she want and what can you do to alleviate the discomfort? This demonstrates empathy. Further empathy is shown when you can acknowledge your spouse's feelings of distress and dissatisfaction.

In the presence of unfocused anger that appears to be displaced on you, you want to exhibit respect, even though you may feel like telling the person what they can do with their anger. If the car mechanic starts castigating you for what happened to your car, turn the anger away by complimenting him or her on his or her skill. This shows respect, and it is hard to stay angry as someone who gives you a compliment. If the anger doesn't stop completely, it will at least subside and probably sputter out.

If you want to defuse anger use any of the techniques described in the preceding paragraphs. In summary:
—Do not get defensive.
—Keep your body language neutral.
—Keep the tone of your voice quiet and reasonable.
—Ask for help.
—Agree.
—Do not accuse.
—Do not threaten.
—Do not deny.
—Apologize.
—Question gently.
—Give feedback.
—Look and act interested.
—Try to problem solve.

—Show respect.
—Compliment.

——284 · Recognize Flashback Reactions

When you find yourself overreacing or unable to be good na-
tured in times of stress or having temper tantrums over minor
irritations, you need to look at what is happening that reminds
you of unpleasant and unwanted past experiences. If you overreact to authority, it may be because your parents belittled you
when you were in their care. If you cannot tolerate good-na-
tured teasing it may be because you were taunted by siblings,
neighborhood children, or schoolmates, and the old feelings of
shame and powerlessness overwhelm you. If stress brings out
your anger it may be because the circumstances of your growing
up evolved around stress-filled scenes that always kept you feeling nervous, on edge, and expecting disaster. If you blow your
stack if an item is left off the shopping list, or someone doesn't
call at the promised time, you are probably responding to old
tapes of neglect and feelings of no one caring about you. Trace
these strong emotions to their roots. When your anger starts,
try to remember what happened to you in the past that reminds
you of what is happening to you now. When you feel your anger
build, remind yourself that what is happening now is happening to an adult who has control. You are no longer a child and
at the mercy of your parents, friends, or teachers. You can
make sure the situation does not get to the point at which it
exceeds your tolerance. Recalling that you are an adult and can
manage as an adult may be all the discipline you need to curb
behavior based on flashbacks to the past instead of reactions to
what is occurring in the present.

——285 · Treasure Your Time

Pretend that this is your last day on earth. Do you want to be
remembered as a hostile person? How would you act if you
wanted to make the most of all that is good in your life? How
does it feel to be appreciative, trusting, relaxed, supportive, and
pleasant? See how the changes you make in yourself cause

others to change how they react to you and how they treat you. Notice how much better it is.

If you were able to enjoy your "last day," always remember that you can control your anger while concentrating on the better aspects of your life. This is proof that you can contain your anger when it is appropriate to the situation. Your anger can be postponed to a time when it is suitable or convenient. You can put it off five minutes. Try putting it off for an hour. Put if off until you can make a rational decision about how you want to deal with it.

286 · Watch Your Language

Do not exaggerate your language to make the situation and your feelings more intense than they are. Don't say that you are going to kill the person. Don't say that he or she is killing you. Words that overstate your feelings incite your actions and encourage behavior that is too strong for the circumstance. Be more precise in labeling what is happening to you and what you plan to do about it. Avoid calling anything a disaster, horrible beyond words or belief, if it is not that terrible. Observe. Do not enlarge on what you see. Stick to what is factual.

287 · See Their Point of View

Everyone has his or her own frame of reference. The person you are disagreeing with may be arguing from an altogether different premise than you are. Try to figure out the other person's point of view. You may be looking at the same thing in different ways because of diverse backgrounds, experiences, beliefs, traditions, and training. Instead of defending your ideas as the only right ones, open yourself up to learning and understanding. Instead of being angry you will be educated.

288 · Try Trust

If you are running around with a chip on your shoulder expecting everyone to challenge you, you are in a state of chronic anger. If you suspect that everyone is trying to take advantage of you, you are a confirmed cynic. If you question everyone's motives, you are unable to trust. It is not recommended that you blindly and naively accept everyone and everything without thought or evaluation. It is recommended that you allow yourself the freedom that trusting others will give you. Try it. Experiment with trust. Let your suspicions and animosities subside while you let others do their jobs and expect them to do right by you. Test trust in some low-risk situations.

—Let the ticket agent select your seat for you. You will get an acceptable seat.[4]

—Let your friend plan a social event without consulting you. You will have a good time.

—Accept an assignment at work just because the work has to be done. Do not check to see if others received similar assignments.

—Do not question the honesty of the excuse your relative made for forgetting your birthday.

—Do not balance your bank statement for one month.

—Let the person who mows your lawn work unsupervised.

—If someone offers to do something for you, accept the offer with thanks. Do not look for ulterior motives.

—Go out on a blind date. Have a good time.

—When working with another person, trust the person to do his or her fair share.

—Loan one of your possessions to somebody. Do not worry about not getting it back or having it broken.

—Hire an expert, such as an accountant, attorney, house painter, and then trust his or her expertise to do the job.

—Vote for the candidate you believe in.

—Trust your daughter to do her homework.

—Ask someone to do you a small favor.

289 · Break Something

You may be the type of person who feels better if you can take your anger out on something. If that sounds like you, you will find it somehow satisfying to break something. It is not a good idea to put holes in the wall or throw the telephone, so stock up in preparation for anger that has to be expressed through destruction. Buy dishes at the thrift store or save glass jars. When the time comes to physically express your anger gather up your crockery collection and shatter it against the wall of the garage. If it further helps your anger you can pick up the shattered pieces, or you can line the area with trash cans to catch the debris.

Stockpile old clothes and rags you can rip or cut. Save newspapers or magazines you can tear apart.

———290 · Assess the Situation

Every instance is not worthy of your anger. For example, if a rude person is drunk your best bet is to walk away. Don't bother getting upset with someone who does not know what he or she is doing.

If children are rude, consider the maturity and the knowledge level of the little people. Maybe they do not know better and need guidance rather than an angry reaction.

If a group of individuals is being annoying and inconsiderate, recognize that their rowdiness is related to the high spirits of the crowd and is not aimed at you. It is better to let them wear down or remove yourself from their presence.

———291 · Things Cannot Always Go Your Way

Do you get upset when things do not go your way? This is normal. But it is a truism that things cannot always go as you would like them to. You are not going to like it when they do not, but you will have more contentment if you face the fact that you will not consistently have your way, that everything will not turn out as you planned it, that you won't get everything you want, and that others will put their interests before yours. When you learn to live with these facts you will react less with anger and more with understanding and acceptance.

———292 · Watch Soap Operas

Soap operas on television are not going to curb your feelings of anger, but they will give you lots of examples of various ways to handle anger. One researcher analyzed thirteen soap operas to find out how the characters dealt with their anger. She found that the actors frequently got angry and expressed their anger without resorting to physical or verbal abuse. Nothing terrible happened to any of the people who got angry. The shows demonstrated that anger was often the emotion used to express hurt, loneliness, and fear. So, one way to educate yourself about anger is to tune in and observe closely. You may find some techniques that will work for you. Note that this advice says to watch soap operas to see examples of positive results from expressing anger. You will not see this in prime time as those characters use violence and vengeance when they are angry.

293 · Let Anger Motivate You

Your anger at your boss may motivate you to get a different job or to open your own business. Anger disrupts complacency. It can move you in the direction you meant to go anyway. It may be the push you need to correct some of the problems in your workplace, your life, your community, or the country. Anger at the status quo has stimulated people to run for public office, campaign to change laws, and set up organizations to serve consumers, the needy, and the abused. Anger has gotten people back to school to learn more about something they care about. Anger has inspired people to start self-help groups for others who share their hurt and distress. There is righteous anger over apparent wrongs. This causes individuals to act to correct the wrongs. If they hadn't cared, they would not have gotten angry. If they hadn't been angry, they would not have acted to change the situation.

294 · Suffer Together

You will often not be the only one who is angry about something. Talk with your fellow sufferers. Be angry together. When you are all in it concurrently you can support each other and moderate each other's feelings. Parallel grumbling is satisfying as all the grousers have their anger in common. There will be many different examples of handling anger in the group. Some

215

will joke, others will cry. There will be those who threaten and those who want to get even. Some will want to pacify and some will want to confront. Commiserate together, but manage your anger in the way you want to, not in the way someone else wants you to.

295 · Wear a Reminder

A visual and ever-present reminder may help you to better manage your anger. One technique is to put a colored dot on your watch face.[5] Buy stick-on red, orange, blue, green, or yellow dots and write a reminder on it so it is there for you to see every time you glance at your wrist. If you want to remind yourself to feel anger you might write "notice" on the dot. If you want to remind yourself not to explode you could print a "no" on the dot. This method makes you always aware and alert to your anger.

296 · Write a Letter

When you are so angry you do not know what to say or how to handle it, or you are unable to tell the person about your anger, write a letter. Follow a format.

1. State how angry you are. Use strong language.
2. State why you are angry. Include everything.
3. Tell the person what you want him or her to do.

Do not mail the letter. This is a method for formulating your anger, knowing your feelings, and determining what you want to happen. Now decide on a constructive way to get what you want. Can you tell the person how you feel and what you want? Do you want to pursue it? How else will the person know how you feel and what you want if you do not tell him or her? The letter helped you put your anger in words. Now you can use the words to tell the person.

297 · Healing Feeling[6]

Anger tucked neatly away is anger that continues to disturb. Go back to your old anger and allow yourself to feel that anger now. Once you have experienced it in the present, you can put it in the past. It is a healing feeling that will allow you to go on without your built-up emotional hurts. How far back do you go? You go back as far as you can remember. Do you have anger with parents, siblings, teachers, friends, or spouses? Get it out. Experience it as though you were the age you were when it happened. Then look at it from an adult perspective, know that it no longer is a feeling that needs to encumber you. Move beyond it. Experiencing the feeling does not mean that the incident is erased from your memory. But the incident has been faced and experienced in a way that allows you to heal. If you do not have the feeling, you will not have the healing. You will grow beyond the feeling if you reach back and go through it. The feeling will grow in you if you do not meet it head on.

Gregory was chronically angry, but he was particularly sensitive whenever he felt he was being criticized or ridiculed in a group. The slightest sense of rejection, or the merest difference of opinion would ruin the encounter for him and send him into a depression. Gregory stuffed his anger away instead of working with it, and he became depressed. He always felt threatened in a group because he expected to be hurt. Because of his anticipation and fear, the depression would sometimes start before he got into the situation. When Gregory applied himself to tracking down this problem he found himself having an emotional reaction to the way he was treated by his family when he was growing up. His family held weekly family council meetings. He and his three siblings would meet with his parents to discuss the week and make decisions on what to do about their problems. They used this time to plan one fun event. He was the youngest person in the family. The meetings became a source of special attention and special embarrassment for him. As the youngest, he was frequently criticized by his siblings for being a pest, getting in their way, and doing stupid things. This was special, albeit negative attention. When the time came for problem solving or suggesting a family event, his ideas were frequently met with derision. Whenever he opened his mouth, his brothers and sisters would groan. As he recalled those weekly ordeals, he felt a wave of anger and shame, but switched immediately to feeling depressed. He stopped himself and focused on all he could recall about the meetings and the mockery he received and made himself feel the unfairness, the powerlessness, the lack of acceptance, the disgrace. He got good and angry. He said what he felt. He said how he should have been treated. He wrote letters to his brothers and sisters and parents. He tore them up, but he did tell them how he felt about how he was treated the next time he saw them. He did not expect them to understand how he felt, and they did not, as they had not been trying to give him a lifelong problem. But he felt better for facing the feeling. He knew where his displaced distress came from. He could then deal with it from an adult point of view and learn new ways to handle group situations. He could dispose of his chronic anger. He no longer expected others to snicker whenever he had an idea. He did not keep looking for signs that others were blaming him for everything. When the old feelings popped up he reminded himself that he was no longer a child at the mercy of those who were older and more powerful than he was. He was an adult and could take care of himself in any encounter with his peers.

———298 · Pretend It Is Someone Else

Disassociating yourself is not recommended, but it sometimes helps to draw back from an anger-filled situation. One technique for doing this is to pretend it is happening to someone else. This allows you to be an observer, to be more objective, and to analyze the reactions and the reasons for them. If you need to do this to get a grip on your anger, it is a useful short-term technique. It can be used to help you understand your anger, but cannot be used long-term as a way to manage your anger.

———299 · Say Ouch

When someone hits you, you say ouch. When you trip or fall you get the ouch feeling. Think of anger in the same vain. When you are insulted it hurts. Say ouch. When you say ouch you are noticing your anger. When you say ouch you are pausing to decide how to respond when you are in an anger-inducing position. You may decide to say, "Ouch, that hurts!" out loud.

——300 · Fight Fair

One way to make your anger work for you is to use your anger to address problems by stating complaints and calling for change. If it only were as simple as that sentence implies. Of course, it isn't that easy. If you point out problems and want a change, you are likely to be angry yourself and the person with whom you are speaking is probably angry too. So follow some rules. Even if you are the only one who follows the rules, you will still have a more successful dispute.

1. Do not be paranoid.

Don't accuse your boss of giving the promotion to your co-worker because she was bribed. Don't tell your spouse that you know she did not want to go to the party because she did not want to see you have a good time. Don't indict your neighbors for making noise in the night just because they knew you had to get up early and needed your sleep.

2. Accept responsibility.

It is not your supervisor's fault that you were away from the office when an important client called. Your spouse is not to blame for your failure to fix the fence before the dogs got out and bit the mailperson. It makes no sense to denounce your neighbors for turning everyone against you.

3. Don't analyze.

Don't tell your boss that he is afraid of your competence and that is why he picks on you. Your spouse won't be more cooperative if you try to make him understand that he is treating you like a child because he feels threatened by your ability. Your neighbor won't be in a problem-solving frame of mind if you tell her that she is jealous of you because you have more than she has.

4. Don't put it off.

If you are feeling a slight at work, don't stew and fester while you imagine what it is. Find out whether or not you have a problem as soon as you can. If your spouse arranges a get-together after you tell him you never want to go anywhere with those people again, deal with the issue before you go, rather than gather up more anger before it is discussed. If your neighbor mows the lawn before you get up, thrash out the annoyance with her before you are ready to inflict bodily harm.

5. Figure out what you want.

Do you want a raise, a promotion, less work, more recognition? Don't fight unless you know what you are fighting for. Do you want your spouse to stop something, start something, or change something? Don't be bad-tempered because you are dissatisfied. Have a goal, a request, a reason, a cause for battle. You may not like your neighbor, but that does not mean you need to fight with him. You may want him never to step on your property again. If that is the case, you know where the argument is going because you know what you want.

6. Stay on the subject.

You are fighting for more vacation time. Your boss says that he doesn't like the number of times you were late to work last year. Refuse to be sidetracked. Bring the subject back to vacation time.

You want to go out to dinner once a month. Your spouse talks about how you waste time. Do not defend yourself or agree. Get back to the purpose of the argument. Talk about the plans for dining out.

You want your neighbor to bring in her garbage cans before she goes to work. She tells you that your garage needs painting. You tell her that she should not be burning tree limbs in her back yard. Get back to what you want. You won't get it by confronting each other about accumulated concerns.

7. Do not bring up the past.

If your boss complains that you have been rude to the new secretary and adds that he did not like the way you treated him when he first came to work at the organization, steer him back to the problem with the secretary. How you treated your boss in the past is another issue.

When your spouse says you forgot to bring home the milk and goes on to complain about the time you forgot to pick up the airplane tickets, and mentions that you once forgot the children at day care, remember that the present problem is the milk. The past problems were discussed when they occurred.

Don't expect your neighbor to discuss his junk car in the driveway with you calmly if you tally up all his past sins, like the time he worked on a boat in his backyard for three years until it became infested with termites and carpenter ants that eventually invaded your house.

8. Stay away from the sensitive stuff.

You have areas of sensitivity. So has everyone else. It is not fighting fair if you throw these in to hurt and confuse. Don't remind your boss that when you were her coworker you knew that she never had any success with men. Your spouse does not need to be told that she has skinny legs and should never wear shorts. Your neighbor knows he is having problems with his children, but doesn't want to hear it from you. You may score a point by bringing up your opponents' sore spots, but you will not be furthering your own interests. They will hold it against you and feel more angry and resolve to be uncooperative.

9. Don't make empty threats.

Don't tell your boss that you are going to quit, your spouse that you are leaving, or your neighbor that you are reporting her, unless you mean it. They will expect you to fulfill your threats, or they will stop hearing them. If you have an ultimatum, make sure it is one you want to enforce should you not get your way.

10. Listen.

Make sure you hear what your adversaries are saying. If you don't listen and they don't either you will both yell louder to get through. If they know you are paying attention they will get to the discussion stage much faster.

11. When the fight is over, stop fighting.

When it is settled, it is settled. If you want to renegotiate, be up front and say so. Don't snipe. Don't pout. Don't start it up again.

——301 · Fight Your Own Fights

You do not want to get sucked in on other people's anger. And it is not good for you to get others to act out your anger. Don't do battle for others. Don't get others to do battle for you. Fight your own fights.

Molly was the newest employee in a company that had many disgruntled workers. The majority of workers were angry with the boss, did not like the personnel policies, and felt they were not secure in their jobs. Molly, in an effort to be accepted, listened to the complaints and identified with her coworkers, although she had no quarrel with the administration. She liked her job and felt that everything was going all right for her, but she got swept up in their fight. She signed a petition and went along to meet with the board of directors. Instead of enjoying her new job she was preoccupied with the pursuit of having the grievances righted. She, along with her coworkers, were fired for insubordination. Molly may have had similar complaints after she had been employed in the company for a longer period of time. However, when she acted it was not out of her own conviction and anger, but because she felt pressured by the other employees. She wanted to be liked and be included. She took that course rather than look at what was right for her.

Tyler found it hard to express anger because he was afraid he would be rejected if he did. He always hid his feelings when he was angry. But this did not prevent him from talking about the person who made him angry. When he was upset with his wife, he told his mother. His mother would then contact the wife and try to take care of the problem for him. When he was furious with a coworker he would tattle to the boss. The boss would react to Tyler's inflammatory report and accost the employee. When one of his children claimed his negative attention he informed his wife. She would discipline the child. Tyler avoided all negative situations by making them someone else's problem. Did this make Tyler more popular and keep people from getting angry with him? You had better believe that it did not. Because of his manipulations, people were constantly disgusted with him.

——302 · Admit Mistakes

You will not lose face by saying, "I'm sorry," when you are wrong. You will be respected for admitting it. Don't get angry when you are found wrong. Accept the criticism or the correction. If you do this graciously you will change an unpleasant turn of events into an opportunity for you to demonstrate that you can take censure and learn from it. You will be admired for your ability to do this.

There is skill involved in accepting criticism. You do not want to defend yourself against it, but you do want to ask for more information. In this way you are converting a negative interaction into a positive conversation. Ask for an example. Show your concern and interest. Then listen. Ask for help. Clarify what you heard by giving feedback or rephrasing. The person criticizing you will be forever grateful that you took it so well. And you will have a technique for using criticism for your benefit. You will save yourself a great deal of unnecessary emotional turmoil.

─── 303 • Use the Person's Name

You are trained to hear your own name. In an argument you are more likely to get a response instead of a reaction if you use the person's name. This will get the individual's attention and make the heated discussion seem more personal and pointed. He or she may start to talk more rationally and with less antagonism. Use this method when dealing with criticism too. Because the criticizer attends to his or her name he or she will take more care in what is said.

For more help see Chapter 5 Lack of Self-Confidence and Chapter 3 Stress.

• NOTES •

1. Dan Kiley. *What to Do When He Won't Change* (New York: G.P. Putnam's Sons, 1987).
2. Judith Martin. "The Proper Way for Polite Persons to Insult Others," *The News Tribune,* 19 May 1985.
3. Carol Tavris. *Anger: The Misunderstood Emotion* (New York: Simon & Schuster, 1982).
4. Redford Williams. *The Trusting Heart: Great News About Type A Behavior* (New York: Times Books, 1989).
4. Dorothy Sarnoff. *Never Be Nervous Again* (New York: Crown Publishers, Inc., 1987).
5. Patricia Love. *The Emotional Incest Syndrome: What To Do When a Parent's Love Rules Your Life* (New York: Bantam Books, 1990).

THE CROSSROAD
COUNSELING LIBRARY
Books of Related Interest

James Archer, Jr.
COUNSELING COLLEGE STUDENTS
A Practical Guide for Teachers, Parents, and Counselors
"Must reading for everyone on campus—professors, administrators, dorm personnel, chaplains, and friends—as well as parents and other counselors to whom college students turn for support."—*Dr. William Van Ornum*
$17.95

Robert W. Buckingham
CARE OF THE DYING CHILD
A Practical Guide for Those Who Help Others
"Buckingham's book delivers a powerful, poignant message deserving a wide readership."—*Library Journal* $17.95

Sidney Callahan
PARENTS FOREVER
You and Your Adult Children
An award-winning writer, psychologist, and mother of six adult children offers reassurance and wisdom to millions of other parents who never knew it would go on for so long. $19.95

David A. Crenshaw
BEREAVEMENT
Counseling the Grieving throughout the Life Cycle
Grief is examined from a life cycle perspective, infancy to old age. Special losses and practical strategies for frontline caregivers highlight this comprehensive guidebook. $17.95 hardcover $10.95 paperback

Paul J. Curtin
HIDDEN RICHES
Stories of ACOAs on the Journey of Recovery
A book of hope and healing for every ACOA or for anyone who knows and loves someone who grew up in a dysfunctional family.
$8.95 paperback

Paul J. Curtin
TUMBLEWEEDS
A Therapist's Guide to Treatment of ACOAs
A book for those who are ACOAs and for those who wish to help ACOAs in their search to experience and share themselves honestly.
$7.95 paperback

Paul J. Curtin
RESISTANCE AND RECOVERY
For Adult Children of Alcoholics
The ideal companion to *Tumbleweeds, Resistance and Recovery* shows how resistance is vital and necessary to recovery when obstacles are turned into growth opportunities. $7.95 paperback

Eugen Drewermann
DISCOVERING THE ROYAL CHILD WITHIN
A Spiritual Psychology of The Little Prince
A depth psychologist, Drewermann sheds light on a beloved symbol and helps readers find new faith in reality. $10.95 paperback

Reuben Fine
THE HISTORY OF PSYCHOANALYSIS
New Expanded Edition
"Objective, comprehensive, and readable. A rare work. Highly recommended."—*Contemporary Psychology* $24.95 paperback

Raymond B. Flannery, Jr.
POST-TRAUMATIC STRESS DISORDER
The Victim's Guide to Healing and Recovery
The first book written for the victim of PTSD that offers specific recovery. $19.95

Raymond B. Flannery, Jr.
BECOMING STRESS-RESISTANT
Through the Project SMART Program
"An eminently practical book with the goals of helping men and women of the 1990s make changes in their lives."—*Charles V. Ford, Academy of Psychosomatic Medicine* $12.95 paperback

Lucy Freeman
FIGHT AGAINST FEARS
With a new Introduction by Flora Rheta Schreiber
More than a million copies sold. The first, and still best, true story of a modern woman's journey of self-discovery through psychoanalysis. $10.95 paperback

Lucy Freeman
OUR INNER WORLD OF RAGE
Understanding and Transforming the Power of Anger
A psychoanalytic examination of the anger that burns within us and which can be used to save or slowly destroy us. $9.95 paperback

Rosemary Ellen Guiley
THE ENCYCLOPEDIA OF DREAMS: SYMBOLS AND INTERPRETATIONS
This comprehensive encyclopedia suggests meanings our dream symbols may have, and guidelines for interpreting the symbols according to our individual lives. $27.50

Virginia Curran Hoffman
THE CODEPENDENT CHURCH
From Dysfunctional Religious Family to Genuine Faith Community
How to recognize and overcome one's codependence on a religious group
through a twelve-step process of spiritual understanding.
$11.95 paperback

Marion Howard
HOW TO HELP YOUR TEENAGER
POSTPONE SEXUAL INVOLVEMENT
This book advises parents, teachers, and counselors on how they can help
their teens resist social and peer pressures regarding sex. $9.95 paperback

Marylou Hughes
THE NURSING HOME EXPERIENCE
A Family Guide to Making it Better
A book of encouragement and answers to help relatives before, during,
and after the difficult nursing home experience. $17.95

Marylou Hughes
MARRIAGE COUNSELING
An Essential Handbook
Concise, practical, and up-to-date—an effective guide to counseling
individuals, couples, and groups. $17.95

Eugene Kennedy
CRISIS COUNSELING
The Essential Guide for Nonprofessional Counselors
"An outstanding author of books on personal growth selects types of
personal crises that our present life-style has made commonplace and
suggests effective ways to deal with them."—*Best Sellers* $10.95

Eugene Kennedy and Sara Charles, M. D.
ON BECOMING A COUNSELOR
A Basic Guide for Nonprofessional Counselors
New expanded edition of an indispensable resource. A patient-oriented,
clinically directed field guide to understanding and responding to
troubled people. $27.95 hardcover $15.95 paperback

Judith M. Knowlton
HIGHER POWERED
A Ninety Day Guide to Serenity and Self-Esteem
"A treasure! Not only those in recovery, but everyone seeking peace and
self-assurance will benefit from the ideas and inspiration in this excellent
book."—*Thomas W. Perrin* $9.95 paperback

Bonnie Lester
WOMEN AND AIDS
A Practical Guide for Those Who Help Others
Provides positive ways for women to deal with their fears, and to help
others who react with fear to people who have AIDS. $15.95

Helen B. McDonald and Audrey I. Steinhorn
UNDERSTANDING HOMOSEXUALITY
A Guide for Those Who Know, Love, or Counsel Gay and Lesbian Individuals
A sensitive guide to better understanding and counseling gay men,
lesbians, and their parents, at every stage of their lives. $10.95 paperback

Mark McGarrity
A GUIDE TO MENTAL RETARDATION
*A Comprehensive Resource for Parents, Teachers, and Helpers who Know, Love,
and Care for People with Mental Retardation at Every Stage of Their Lives*
A valuable reference. $24.95

James McGuirk and Mary Elizabeth McGuirk
FOR WANT OF A CHILD
A Psychologist and His Wife Explore the Emotional
Effects and Challenges of Infertility
A new understanding of infertility that comes from one couple's lived
experience, as well as sound professional advice for couples and
counselors. $17.95

Janice N. McLean and Sheila A. Knights
PHOBICS AND OTHER PANIC VICTIMS
A Practical Guide for Those Who Help Them
"A must for the phobic, spouse and family, and for the physician and
support people who help them."—*Arthur B. Hardy, M. D., Founder,
TERRAP Phobia Program* $17.95

John B. Mordock and William Van Ornum
CRISIS COUNSELING WITH CHILDREN AND ADOLESCENTS
A Guide for Nonprofessional Counselors
New Expanded Edition
"Every parent should keep this book on the shelf right next to the
nutrition, medical, and Dr. Spock books."—*Marriage & Family Living*
$12.95

John B. Mordock
COUNSELING CHILDREN
Basic Principles for Helping the Troubled and Defiant Child
Helps counselors consider the best route for a particular child, and offers
proven principles and methods to counsel troubled children in a variety
of situations. $17.95

William F. Nerin
YOU CAN'T GROW UP TILL YOU GO BACK HOME
A Safe Journey to See Your Parents as Human
How understanding our roots and accepting our parents as persons, can
bring peace, self-esteem, and understanding. $21.95

Cherry Boone O'Neill
DEAR CHERRY
Questions and Answers on Eating Disorders
Practical and inspiring advice on eating disorders from the best- selling
author of *Starving for Attention*. $8.95 paperback

Thomas W. Perrin
I AM AN ADULT WHO GREW UP IN AN ALCOHOLIC FAMILY
At once moving and practical, this long-awaited book by a leader in the
addiction field provides new hope to other adult children of alcoholics and
those who love them. $8.95 paperback

Dianne Doyle Pita
ADDICTIONS COUNSELING
A Practical Guide to Counseling People
with Chemical and Other Addictions
"A fresh and greatly needed approach to helping the whole person—it fills
a great gap in the existing literature."—*Thomas Perrin* $17.95

Paul G. Quinnett
SUICIDE: THE FOREVER DECISION
For Those Thinking About Suicide,
and For Those Who Know, Love, or Counsel Them
New Expanded Edition
"A treasure— this book can help save lives."—*William Van Ornum,
psychotherapist and author* $9.95 paperback

Paul G. Quinnett
WHEN SELF-HELP FAILS
A Consumer's Guide to Counseling Services
"Without a doubt one of the most honest, reassuring, nonpaternalistic,
and useful self-help books ever to appear."—*Booklist* $11.95 paperback

Judah L. Ronch
ALZHEIMER'S DISEASE
A Practical Guide for Families and Other Caregivers
Must reading for everyone who must deal with the effects of this tragic
disease on a daily basis. $11.95 paperback

Theodore Isaac Rubin, M. D.
CHILD POTENTIAL
Fulfilling Your Child's Intellectual, Emotional, and Creative Promise
Information, guidance, and wisdom—a treasury of fresh ideas for parents
to help their children become their best selves.
$17.95 hardcover $11.95 paperback

E. Fritz Schmerl, M. D. with Sally Patterson Tubach
THE CHALLENGE OF AGE
A Guide to Growing Older in Health and Happiness
"A practical, commonsensical guide for all ages."—*Booklist*
$14.95 paperback